CW00523901

MINORITY SHAREHOLDERS' RIGHTS

AUSTRALIA AND NEW ZEALAND
The Law Book Company Ltd.
Sydney : Melbourne : Perth

CANADA AND U.S.A.
The Carswell Company Ltd.
Agincourt, Ontario

INDIA
N.M. Tripathi Private Ltd.
Bombay
and
Eastern Law House Private Ltd.
Calcutta and Delhi
M.P.P. House
Bangalore

ISRAEL
Steimatzky's Agency Ltd.
Jerusalem : Tel Aviv : Haifa

PAKISTAN
Pakistan Law House
Karachi

MINORITY SHAREHOLDERS' RIGHTS

BY

ROBIN HOLLINGTON
M.A. (Oxon.), LL.M. (Penn.),
of Lincoln's Inn, Barrister

with a foreword by The Honourable Mr. Justice Hoffmann

LONDON
SWEET & MAXWELL
1990

Published in 1990 by
Sweet & Maxwell Limited of
South Quay Plaza, 183 Marsh Wall,
London E14 9FT
Phototypeset by
LBJ Enterprises Limited
Chilcompton, Somerset
Printed in Great Britain by
Butler and Tanner of
Frome, Somerset

British Library Cataloguing in Publication Data

Hollington, Robin
Minority Shareholders' Rights
1. Great Britain. Companies. Shareholding. Law
I. Title
344.106666

ISBN 0–421–40740–9

FOREWORD

The emancipation of minority shareholders is a recent event. For most of the first century of company law they were virtually defenceless, kept in cowed submission by a fire-breathing and possibly multiple-headed dragon called *Foss* v. *Harbottle.* Only in exceptional cases could they claim the protection of the court. A statutory remedy was provided for the first time in 1948 but this proved relatively ineffectual. It was not until 1980 that Parliament forged the sword which is now section 459 of the Companies Act 1985 and which enables the unfairly treated minority shareholder to slay the dragon.

The rights of minority shareholders is an important and rapidly developing branch of law. It raises difficult questions of principle: the conflicts between the letter and the spirit of the company's constitution; between the sanctity of the bargain between shareholders embodied in the articles and the prevention of unfair treatment; between giving a remedy which is effective and allowing it to become an instrument of abuse; between the attainment of fairness and the amount of money which the parties can afford to spend on litigation.

All these questions are lucidly expounded in this book, which deals comprehensively with the law and procedure of minority shareholder's remedies. There are of course chapters on these topics in the standard works on company law but nothing which discusses the principles and the authorities as fully as Mr. Hollington has done.

L. H. H. Hoffmann

PREFACE

The purpose of this short book is to identify and analyse those circumstances in which minority shareholders in companies can escape from the general principle of majority rule. There are several relevant threads of judicial precedent and statute, some of respectable antiquity (such as "the rule in *Foss* v. *Harbottle*") and others of unproven modernity (such as the unfair prejudice remedy in section 459 of the Companies Act 1985). An attempt is made here to draw those threads together so far as possible. For no reason other than ease of exposition, the book largely follows a chronological course.

The law relating to minority shareholders is developing and changing rapidly. Hardly a month passes without an important new case. *Re Abbey Leisure* (C.A., *The Times,* December 19, 1989) is a recent decision on the just and equitable winding-up remedy, which raises more questions than it answers. Consideration is currently being given to amending the Rules of the Supreme Court so as to make express provision for derivative actions. It is understood that the current proposal requires a plaintiff to apply for leave to continue his derivative action, at which stage the court can give directions for, *inter alia,* the holding of meetings and in relation to costs. The Companies Act 1989 makes changes, *inter alia,* in relation to official powers of investigation.

This book is also written against a backcloth of proposals for fundamental change to (some might say, the "Americanisation" of) the structure of the legal profession and the administration of justice. For example, it is proposed that the prohibition against contingency fees be relaxed so as to increase access to the courts. The availability of legal aid is part of the same political debate. If the prohibition against contingency fees is relaxed, this may have a very significant impact on the law and practice relating to derivative actions. It is no coincidence that contingency fees are commonly used in jurisdictions in the United States to pursue derivative actions. In England, not only are contingency fees outlawed, but also legal aid is not available to fund derivative actions. The courts are already faced with the mighty task of preventing the allegedly oppressed (and their lawyers) becoming the oppressors, a task which no doubt will be made even more difficult as access to the courts is increased by one means or another.

I would like to express my thanks to the editorial staff of Sweet & Maxwell, past and present, for their very great assistance, not to mention patience, in the course of the writing of this book.

The law is stated as at December 20, 1989.

Robin Hollington
Lincoln's Inn
London

CONTENTS

		page
Foreword		v
Preface		vii
Table of Cases		xi
Table of Statutes		xvi
Table of Rules		xviii
CHAPTER 1	Introduction	1
CHAPTER 2	Equitable exceptions to the general principle of majority rule	3
CHAPTER 3	Winding-up on the just and equitable ground	29
CHAPTER 4	The unfair prejudice remedy	45
CHAPTER 5	Personal rights of shareholders	83
CHAPTER 6	Miscellaneous rights of individual shareholders	97
APPENDIX		105
Index		[113]

TABLE OF CASES

Abbey Leisure Ltd., *Re* (1989) 5 B.C.C. 183 .... 4–054, 4–057, 4–060, 4–061
Allen *v*. Gold Reefs [1900] 1 Ch.D. 656 6–005
Allen *v*. Hyatt (1914) 30 TLR 444 5–020
American Cyanamid *v*. Ethicon Ltd. [1975] A.C. 396; [1975] 2 W.L.R. 316; 119 S.J. 136; [1975] 1 All E.R. 504; [1975] F.S.R. 101; [1975] R.P.C. 513, H.L.; reversing [1974] F.S.R. 312, C.A. 4–017, 4–019
Automatic Self-Cleansing Filter Syndicate *v*. Cuninghame [1906] 2 Ch. 34 2–014

Bamford *v*. Bamford [1970] Ch. 212; [1969] 2 W.L.R. 1107; 113, S.J. 123; [1969] 1 All E.R. 969; [32 M.L.R. 563], C.A. affirmiing [1968] 3 W.L.R. 317; 112 S.J. 416; [1968] 2 All E.R. 655; [31 M.L.R. 688]; [1968] C.L.Y. 441 5–009, 5–021, 5–022, 5–023
Barron *v*. Potter [1914] 1 Ch. 895 3–024
Beddoe, *Re;* Downes *v*. Cottam [1893] 1 Ch. 547 2–037
Bellador Silk Ltd., *Re* [1965] 1 W.L.R. 1051; [1965] 1 All E.R. 667; [109 S.J. 1019; 29 M.L.R. 321] 4–001
Bentley-Stevens *v*. Jones [1974] 1 W.L.R. 638; 1185 S.J. 345; [1974] 2 All E.R. 653 5–006
Birch *v*. Sullivan [1957] 1 W.L.R. 1247; 101 S.J. 974; [1958] 1 All E.R. 56 2–042
Bird Precision Bellows, *Re* [1986] Ch. 658; [1986] 2 W.L.R. 158; (1986) 130 S.J. 51; [1985] 3 All E.R. 523; (1986) 83 L.S.Gaz. 36; [1986] PCC 25 C.A.; affirming [1984] Ch. 419; [1984] 2 W.L.R. 869; (1984) 128 S.J. 348; [1984] 3 All E.R. 444; (1984) 81 L.S.Gaz. 187 .... 4–037, 4–038, 4–049, 4–052, 4–061, 4–067, 4–068
Boswell (Steels) & Co. Ltd., *Re* (1989) 5 B.C.C. 145 4–050
Blue Arrow plc, *Re* [1987] B.C.L.C. 585 4–029
Bovey Hotel Ventures Ltd., *Re,* unreported C.A. July 31, 1981 4–033,4–040
Breckland Group *v*. London and Suffolk Properties [1989] B.C.L.C. 100 2–014
Bugle Press Ltd., *Re* Application of H.C. Treby, *Re* Houses and Estates [1961] Ch. 270; [1960] 3 W.L.R. 956; 104 S.J. 1057; [1960] 3 All E.R. 791; [77 L.Q.R. 9] C.A., Affirming [1961] Ch. 270; [1960] 2 W.L.R. 658; 104 S.J. 289; [1960] 1 All E.R. 768; [76 L.Q.R. 344; 23 M.L.R. 663; 143 Acct. 440] 6–011
Burland *v*. Earle [1901] A.C. 83 2–022
Bushell *v*. Faith [1970] A.C. 1099; [1970] 2 W.L.R. 272; 114 S.J. 54; [1970] 1 All E.R. 53, H.L.; affirming [1969] 2 Ch. 438; [1969] 2 W.L.R. 1067; 113 S.J. 262; [1969] 1 All E.R. 1002, C.A.; [86 L.Q.R. 155] 3–017, 6–005

Carrington *v*. Viyella (1983) B.C.C. 98 4–032
Castleburn, *Re* Ltd. (1989) 5 B.C.C. 652 .... 4–049, 4–052, 4–053, 4–061

D. R. Chemicals Ltd. (1989) 5 B.C.C. 39, 53–54 ..... 4–035, 4–036, 4–045, 4–060, 4–071
Chesterfield Catering Co. Ltd., *Re* [1977] Ch. 373 3–012
Claybridge Shipping Co. S.A., *Re,* [1981] Com.L.R. 107, *The Times,* March 14, 1981, C.A. 3–008

Clemens *v.* Clemens Bros. Ltd. [1976] 2 All E.R. 268 .... 2–011, 2–043
Coleman *v.* Myers [1977] 2 N.Z.L.R. 225; 298, N.Z. Sup. Ct. 5–020
Company, A, *Re* [1985] B.C.L.C. 80 4–019
Comany, A, *Re* [1986] B.C.L.C. 68 .... 4–011, 4–065
Company, A, *Re (No. 003843 of 1986)* [1987] B.C.L.C. 562 .... 4–055, 4–067
Company, A, *Re (No. 00370 of 1987) ex p.* Glossop [1988] 1 W.L.R. 1068 2–006, 4–036
Company, A, *Re (No. 003096 of 1987)* (1988) 4 B.C.C. 80 .... 4–036, 4–038, 4–039
Company, A, *Re* (1988) 4 B.C.C. 507 .... 4–036, 4–038
Company, A, *Re (No. 001363 of 1988)* (1989) 5 B.C.C. 18 4–011
Company, A, *Re (No. 002567 of 1982)* [1983] B.C.L.C. 151; [1983] 1 W.L.R. 927; (9183) 127 S.J. 508; [1983] 2 All E.R. 854; (1983) 80 L.S.Gaz. 2133 4–036, 4–057
Company, A, *Re (No. 004475 of 1982)* [1983] Ch. 178; [1983] 2 W.L.R. 381; (1983) 127 S.J. 153; [1983] 2 All E.R. 36 4–027
Company, A, *Re (No. 007623 of 1984)* [1986] B.C.L.C. 362; (1986) 2 B.C.C. 99 . 4–038, 4–046, 4–047, 4–064, 4–070
Company, A, *Re (No. 007828 of 1985)* 4–005
Company, A, *Re (No. 008699 of 1985)* [1986] B.C.L.C. 382; (1986) B.C.C. 99; 1986 PCC 296 4–044
Company, A, *Re (No. 00477 of 1986)* [1986] B.C.L.C. 376; (1986) B.C.C. 99 4–027, 4–036, 4–065
Company, A, *Re (No. 001761 of 1986)* [1987] B.C.L.C. 141 .... 4–022, 4–034
Company, A, *Re (No. 003160 of 1986),* [1986] B.C.L.C. 391; (1986) 2 B.C.C. ... 3–006, 4–007, 4–008, 4–009, 4–028, 4–036
Company, A, *Re (No. 003843 of 1986),* [1987] B.C.L.C. 562 .... 4–055, 4–058, 4–063
Company A, *Re (No. 004175 of 1986)* [1987] 1 W.L.R. 585; (1987) 131 S.J. 690; [1987] B.C.L.C. 574; (1987) 84 L.S.Gaz. 1732 4–020
Company, A, *Re (No. 004377 of 1986),* [1987] 1 W.L.R. 102; (1987) 131 S.J. 132; [1987] B.C.L.C. 94; (1987) 84 L.S.Gaz. 653 .... 4–040, 4–041
Company, A, *Re (No. 007281 of 1986),* (1987) 3 B.C.C. 375; 1987 PCC 403; [1987] B.C.L.C. 593 4–073
Company, A, *Re (No. 00370 of 1987) ex p.* Glossop, *Re* (1988) 4 B.C.C. 507; [1988] 1 W.L.R. 1068 .... 2–006, 3–028, 4–032, 4–043
Company, A, *Re (No. 00789 of 1987)* (1989) 5 B.C.C. 792 .... 4–014, 4–016, 4–033
Company A, *Re (No. 003028 of 1987)* [1988] B.C.L.C. 282 3–034
Company, A, *Re (No. 3096 of 1987)* (1988) 4 B.C.C. 80 .... 3–019, 4–058, 4–060, 4–063
Company, A, *Re (No. 001363 of 1988)* (1989) 5 B.C.C. 18 .... 3–008, 3–033, 4–010
Company, A, *Re (No. 006834 of 1988)* (1989) 5 B.C.C. 218 4–014, 4–038, 4–049, 4–053, 4–060, 4–062, 4–063
Cook *v.* Deeks [1916] 1 A.C. 554 .... 2–022, 2–024, 2–030, 2–031
Coulson Sanderson & Ward Ltd. *v.* Ward [1986] 2 B.C.C. 99 3–032
Crossmore Electrical & Civil Engineering Ltd., *Re* (1989) 5 B.C.C. 37 .... 3–036, 4–074
Cumana, *Re* [1986] B.C.L.C. 430 ...... 3–031, 4–013, 4–019, 4–040, 4–041, 4–045, 4–071
Cumbrian Newspapers *v.* Cumberland and Westmorland Herald Newspapers & Printing Co. [1987] Fam. 1; [1987] Ch. 1; [1986] 3 W.L.R. 26; [1986] B.C.L.C. 286; (1986) 130 S.J. 446; [1986] 2 All E.R. 816; 1987 PCC 12; (1986) 83 L.S.Gaz. 1719 .... 5–014, 6–005, 6–008

Dafen Tinplate *v.* Llanelly Steel [1920] 2 Ch. 124 .... 2–008, 2–010
Daniels *v.* Daniels [1978] Ch. 406; [1978] 2 W.L.R. 73; [1978] 2 All E.R. 89; (1977) 121 S.J. 605 .... 2–023, 2–025, 2–030
Dawson *v.* Coats Paton [1989] B.C.L.C. 233 .... 4–044, 5–025

Ebrahimi *v.* Westbourne Galleries [1973] A.C. 360; [1972] 2 W.L.R. 1289; 116 S.J. 412; [1972] 2 All E.R. 492, H.L. reversing *sub nom.* Westbourne Galleries, *Re* [1971] Ch. 799; [1971] 2 W.L.R. 618; (1970) 115 S.J. 74; [1971] 1 All E.R. 56 C.A.; reversing [1970] 1 W.L.R. 1378; 114 S.J. 785; [1970] 3 All E.R. 374 .... 2–011,2–043, 3–016,3–018, 3–020, 3–022, 3–026, 3–033, 4–009, 4–026, 4–027, 4–036, 4–039, 4–054, 5–014

Edwards *v.* Halliwell [1950] W.N. 537; 94 S.J. 803; [1950] 2 All E.R. 1064; [18 Sol. 40], C.A. 2–040, 5–001, 5–008
Estmancol (Kilner House) Ltd. *v.* G.L.C. [1982] 1 W.L.R. 2 ...... 2–025, 2–030, 2–043
Expanded Plugs Ltd., *Re* [1966] 1 W.L.R. 514; 110 S.J. 246; [1966] 1 All E.R. 877 3–009

Fargro *v.* Godfrey [1986] 1 W.L.R. 1134; [1986] B.C.L.C. 370; (1986) 130 S.J. 524; [1986] 3 All E.R. 279; [1986] PCC 476; (1986) 83 L.S.Gaz. 2326 2–034
Ferguson *v.* Wallbridge [1935] 3 D.L.R. 2–034
Foss *v.* Harbottle (1843) 2 Hare 461; [106 L.J. 611; [1957] C.L.J. 194; [1958] C.L.J. 93; 74 S.A.L.J. 443; 35 M.L.R. 318; 49A L.J. 134; 40 Con*v*. 51 .... 1–001, 1–003, 2–006, 2–017, 2–019, 2–022, 2–024, 2–025, 2–027, 2–029, 2–030, 2–036, 2–040

Garage Door Associates Ltd., *Re* [1984] 1 W.L.R. 35; [1984] 1 All E.R. 434; (1983) 80 L.S.Gaz. 3157 .... 3–008, 4–010
Gray's Inn Construction Co., *Re* [1980] 1 W.L.R. 711; (1979) 124 S.J. 463; [1980] 1 All E.R. 814, C.A. 3–036
Greenhalgh *v.* Arderne Cinemas [1951] Ch. 286; 96 S.J. 855; [1950] 2 All E.R. 1120; [101 L.J. 173; 18 Sol. 40], C.A. 2–006, 2–008, 2–009, 2–010, 2–011, 2–012, 2–019, 2–025, 2–043, 3–016

Halt Garages Ltd., *Re* [1982] 3 All E.R. 1016 4–042
Harmer, *Re* [1959] 1 W.L.R. 62; 103 S.J. 73; [1958] 3 All E.R. 689; [22 M.L.R. 340; [1959] C.L.J. 37; 109 L.J. 147; 103 S.J. 26; 56 Sec. 7], C.A. 4–016
Heron International *v.* Lew Grade [1983] B.C.L.C. 244; [1982] Com. L.R. 108, C.A. 4–044, 5–010, 5–021, 5–023, 5–024, 5–025
Hickman's Case [1915] 1 Ch. 881 .... 5–013, 5–014
Hogg *v.* Cramphorn; Same *v.* Same [1967] Ch. 254; [1966] 3 W.L.R. 995; 110 S.J. 887; [1966] 3 All E.R. 420; [1963] C.L.Y. 397; [30 M.L.R. 77] 5–021

JN 2 Ltd., *Re* [1978] 1 W.L.R. 183; (1977) 121 S.J. 46; [1977] 3 All E.R. .. 3–006, 3–007
Jaybird Group *v.* Greenwood [1986] B.C.L.C. 319 2–038
Jermyn Street Turkish Baths, *Re* [1971] 1 W.L.R. 1042 4–041

Loch *v.* John Blackwood Ltd. [1924] A.C. 783 .... 3–023, 3–026
London School of Electronics, *Re* [1986] Ch. 211; [1985] 3 W.L.R. 474; (1985) 129 S.J. 573; 1985 P.C.C. 248 .... 4–035, 4–037, 4–040, 4–067, 4–071

MacDougall *v.* Gardiner (1875) 1 Ch. 13 5–007
McGuinness, *Re* (1988) B.C.C. 161 .... 4–015, 4–032, 4–033
Marks *v.* Estates & General Investments [1976] 1 W.L.R. 380 4–021
Marshall's Valve Gear Co. Ltd. *v.* Manning Wardle & Co. Ltd. [1909] 1 Ch. 267 . 2–014
Martin Coulter, *Re* [1988] B.C.L.C. 12 3–009
Mason *v.* Harris (1879) 11 Ch. D. 97 2–030
Mozley *v.* Alston 5–007
Multinational *v.* Multinational [1983] Ch. 258 2–024
Noble (Clothing), R.A. Ltd., *Re* [1983] B.C.L.C. 273 3–020, 3–026, 3–032, 4–033, 4–035, 4–036, 4–037, 4–043

North-West Transportation Co. Ltd. *v.* Beatty [1887] 12 App. Cas. 289 .... 2–021, 2–022
Nurcombe *v.* Nurcombe [1985] 1 W.L.R. 370; (1984) 128 S.J. 766; [1985] 1 All E.R. 65; (1984) 81 L.S.Gaz. 2929, C.A. 2–042

O.C. (Transport) Services, Ltd., *Re* [1984] B.C.L.C. 2511 4–067

Pavlides *v.* Jensen [1956] Ch. 565 .... 2–024, 2–025, 2–026, 2–030

Percival *v.* Wright [1902] 2 Ch. 421 5–020
Piercy *v.* Mills [1920] 1 Ch. 77 5–021
Postgate & Denby (Agencies) Ltd., *Re* [1987] B.C.L.C. 8 .... 4–018, 4–029, 4–030
Prudential Assurance *v.* Newman Industries (No. 2) [1981] Ch. 257; [1980] 3 W.L.R. 543; (1980) 124 S.J. 756; [1980] 2 All E.R. 841 .... 2–024, 2–026, 2–027, 2–030, 2–032, 2–033, 2–036, 2–038, 5–016
Punt *v.* Symons [1903] 2 Ch. 506 5–021

Quickdrome, *Re* [1988] B.C.L.C. 370 .... 4–003, 4–008, 4–009
Quinn & Axtens Ltd. *v.* Salmon [1909] 1 Ch. 311 .... 5–010, 5–014

Rayfield *v.* Hands [1960] Ch. 1, [1958] 2 W.L.R. 851; 102 S.J. 348; [1958] 2 All E.R. 194; [1958] C.L.J. 148; 139 Acct. 189; 102 S.J. 390; 21 M.L.R. 401, 657; 22 Con*v*. 315 5–010
Regal (Hastings) *v.* Gulliver [1942] 1 All E.R. 378 .... 2–006, 2–021, 2–024
Rica Gold Washing Co. Ltd., *Re* (1879) 11 Ch.D. 36 .... 3–009, 3–012
Ringtower Holdings plc, *Re* (1989) 5 B.C.C. 82 .... 4–014, 4–032, 4–035, 4–038, 4–063

Scottish Cooperative Wholesale Society Ltd. *v.* Meyer [1959] A.C. 324; [1958] 3 W.L.R. 404; 102 S.J. 617; [1958] 3 All E.R. 66; *sub nom.* Meyer *v.* Scottish Cooperative Wholesale Society, 1958 S.C.(H.L.) 40; [102 S.J. 698; [1958] J.B.L. 404; [1958] C.L.J. 152; 62 Accountants Mag. 699; 75 L.Q.R. 39; 21 M.L.R. 653], H.L.; affirming *sub nom.* Mayer *v.* Scottish Textiles & Manufacturing Co., 1957 S.C. 110; 1957 S.L.T. 250; [54 Sec. 552]; C.L.Y. 437 .... 2–011, 4–023, 4–026, 4–032, 4–033, 4–040, 4–067
Scott's Trustees, *Re* [1959] A.C. 763 4–007
Seaton *v.* Grant [1867] L.R. 2 Ch. App. 459 2–042
Shaw *v.* Shaw [1935] 2 K.B. 113 2–014
Sherborne Park Residents Co. Ltd., *Re* [1987] B.C.L.C. 82 .... 4–021, 5–024
Shuttleworth *v.* Cox [1927] 2 K.B. 9 2–008
Sidebottom *v.* Kershaw, Leese & Co. [1920] 1 Ch. 154 2–008
Simpson *v.* Westminister Palace Hotel (1860) 8 H.L.C. 712 5–011
Smith *v.* Ampol [1974] A.C. 821 5–021
Smith *v.* Croft (No. 1) [1986] 1 W.L.R. 580; (1986) 130 S.J. 314; [1986] 2 All E.R. 551; 1986 PCC 412; [1987] B.C.L.C. 355; [1987] 1 FTLR 319; 1986 PCC 209; (1987) 84 L.S.Gaz. 2449 .... 2–039, 4–042
Smith *v.* Croft (No. 2) [1987] 3 W.L.R. 405; (1987) 131 S.J. 1038; [1987] 3 All E.R. 909; [1987] B.C.L.C. 355; [1987] 1 FTLR 319; 1986 PCC 209; (1987) 84 L.S.Gaz. 2449 .... 1–002, 2–009, 2–030, 2–031, 2–037, 2–039, 2–043, 5–011
Southern Foundries (1926) Ltd. *v.* Shirlaw [1940] A.C. 701 6–005
Stewarts (Brixon) Ltd., *Re* [1985] B.C.L.C. 4–023, 4–040, 4–065
Syers *v.* Syers (1876) 1 App. Cas. 174 4–057

Tay Bok Choon *v.* Tahanson [1987] B.C.L.C. 472; [1987] 1 W.L.R. 413 3–021
Taylor *v.* National Union of Mineworkers (Derbyshire Area) [1985] I.R.L.R. 99; [1985] 1.R.L.R. 65; [1984] I.R.L.R. 440 2–032
Tett *v.* Phoenix Property & Investment Co. 1986 PCC 210; (1985) 129 S.J. 869; (1986) 83 L.S.Gaz. 116, C.A. 5–010
Theakston *v.* London Trust plc [1984] B.C.L.C. 390 4–007

Vujnovich *v.* Vujnovich (1989) 5 B.C.C. 740 3–017

Walker *v.* London Tramways (1879) 12 Ch. D. 705 6–005
Wallersteiner *v.* Moir (No. 2) [1975] Q.B. 373; [1975] 2 W.L.R. 389; 119 S.J. 97; [1975] 1 All E.R. 849; [173 Acct. 154; 40 Con*v*. 51], C.A. 2–037, 2–039
Weller, Sam & Sons Ltd., *Re* (1989) 5 B.C.C. 810 .... 4–032, 4–043

Westbourne Galleries, *Re. See* Ebrahimi *v.* Westbourne Galleries ....
White *v.* Bristol Aeroplane Co. [1953] Ch. 65; [1953] 2 W.L.R. 144; 97 1952. p.504; April, 1953, p.302; 103 L.J. 67; 215 L.T. 299; 69 L.Q.R. 156, C.A.; reversing *The Times,* November 29, 1952 6–009
Wood *v.* Odessa Waterworks Co. (1889) 42 Ch. D. 636 5–010

XYZ Ltd., *Re* [1987] 1 W.L.R. 102 3–019, 4–036, 4–038, 4–039, 4–040, 4–048, 4–050, 4–051, 4–052

Yenidge Tobacco Co. Ltd., *Re* [1916] 2 Ch. 426 3–025

TABLE OF STATUTES

1890 The Partnership Act (c. 39)
s.35 3–023
1948 Companies Act (c.38) 1–003, 2–005
s.210 ..... 1–001, 2–011, 4–001, 4–023, 4–026, 4–041, 4–043
s.222(f) 2–011
1980 Companies Act (c.22)
s.32 6–006
s.75 .... 2–043, 4–019, 4–047
1981 Supreme Court Act (c.54)
s.37 4–017
1984 County Court Act (c.28)
s.38 4–017
1985 Companies Act (c.6) 1–003, 2–005, 3–010, 6–001
Pt. XVII 1–001, 1–002, 1–004, 3–031, 4–001, 4–002, 4–008, 4–019, 4–021, 4–024, 4–031, 4–072
s.2 6–004
s.4 .... 6–002, 6–003
s.5 6–003
s.9 .... 5–005, 6–002, 6–005
(1) 6–005
s.14 6–002
(1) 5–005, 5–006, 5–008, 5–013
s.17 6–004
(2)(b) 6–005
s.22 4–002
s.24 .... 3–004, 3–011
s.54(3) 6–010
(4) 6–010
(5) 6–010
(6) 6–010
(7) 6–010
(8) 6–010
(9) 6–010
(10) 6–010
s.75 4–037
s.89 7–004

Companies Act—*cont.*
s.125 ..... 5–005, 6–006, 6–008, 7–002
(2) 6–006
(3)(c) 6–006
(4) 6–006
(5) 6–006
s.126 6–006
s.127 .... 6–006, 6–007
(4) 6–007
s.155 6–010
s.157(2) 6–010
(3) 6–010
s.173 6–010
s.176 6–010
s.177 6–010
s.183 4–007
s.303 6–005
s.210 4–026
s.359 .... 3–005, 4–003
s.428 6–011
s.429 6–011
s.430 6–011
s.430A(1) 6–012
C(1) 6–011
(3) 6–012
(4) 6–011
F 6–011
s.431 6–013
s.432 6–013
s.433 6–013
s.434 6–013
s.435 6–013
s.436 6–013
s.437 6–013
s.438 6–013
s.439 6–014
s.440 6–014
s.441 6–014
s.459 ..... 2–043, 3–033, 4–002, 4–023, 4–027, 4–060, 6–007

Companies Act—*cont.*
s.459(1) 4–001, 4–002, 4–020
(2) 4–002, 4–004, 4–007, 4–008
s.461 ...... 2–041, 3–030, 7–005
(1) 4–011, 4–020
(2) 4–012, 4–020
(a) 4–020
(d) 4–020
(3) 4–012
(4) 4–012
s.517(1)(g) 4–027
s.738(1) 3–006
1986 Financial Service Act (c.60)
s.172 6–011
Sched. 12 6–011
1986 Insolvency Act (c.45)
s.76 3–004
s.77 3–004
s.78 3–004
s.79 3–004
(1) 3–003
s.80 3–004
s.81 3–004
s.82 3–004
s.122(e) 3–004, 3–011
(1)(g) 3–001
s.124(2) 3–002
(a) 3–004, 3–010
s.125(2) 3–001, 3–002, 3–031
s.127 3–036
s.129(1) 3–004
s.212(5) 2–034

TABLE OF RULES

1983 Civil Courts Order (S.I. 1983 No. 713) 3–035
1986 Companies (Unfair Prejudice Applications) Proceedings Rules (S.I. 1986 No. 2000) 4–072
1986 Insolvency Rules
r.4.22 3–035
r.4.23 3–035
s.4.24 3–035
1981 Rules of the Supreme Court
Ord. 29 4–017

Chapter 1

INTRODUCTION

1–001 Prior to the enactment of section 210 of the Companies Act 1948 ("the 1948 Act") and its successors, culminating in the provisions of Part XVII of the Companies Act 1985 ("the 1985 Act"), the extent of the rights enjoyed by minority shareholders could be said to be determined by "the rule in *Foss* v. *Harbottle*."[1] As will be seen, that "rule" embraced not one but several principles.[2] In so doing it is submitted that the "rule" has resulted in confusion from which the law is beginning to emerge. The principal confusion, it is submitted,[3] has arisen from the misplaced emphasis on formulations of the "rule" on the ratifiability of certain acts by the members in general meeting.

1–002 The rights enjoyed by minority shareholders are now dominated by the provisions of Part XVII of the 1985 Act, and to a lesser extent the provisions relating to the winding-up of companies on the just and equitable ground.[4] It is too early, however, to say whether the "rule" has become a matter of largely historical interest. Recent cases such as *Smith* v. *Croft (No. 2)*[5] suggest that the "rule" retains considerable vitality.

1–003 As will be explored at the beginning of Chapter 2, the "rule," and indeed any principles regarding the rights of minority shareholders, must deal with the two related concepts:

(1) that a company is a legal entity distinct from its corporators (a concept that was new at the time that *Foss* v. *Harbottle* was decided); and
(2) that a group cannot function efficiently (especially important in matters of commerce) unless the will of the majority generally prevails.

[1] (1843) 2 Hare 461.
[2] See paras. 2–012, 5–001 and 5–002.
[3] See paras. 2–018, and 5–011.
[4] See Chaps. 3 and 4 below.
[5] [1988] Ch. 114. See paras. 2–029, etc., and 5–011.

Minority shareholders would be held to have no rights if these concepts were ruthlessly applied. In the case of companies registered under the Companies Acts, the first line of protection for minority shareholders will be the existence of the memorandum and articles of association of the company which will not be freely alterable by a simple majority of members.

1–004 This book is principally concerned with non-quoted companies and the means by which individual shareholders can protect themselves in practice from abuses of power by the majority, whether those abuses are acts of the directors or shareholders. The position of such individual shareholders is distinguished from that of a shareholder in a quoted company by the restricted marketability of the former's shares. Abuse of power in the case of quoted companies is much less likely to have a discernible and direct impact on the value of its shares and disgruntled shareholders can easily realise their investment in the company by selling their shares. A minority shareholding in a non-quoted company is usually not an investment in the same sense: it is undoubtedly an interest of value but its value cannot be assessed by reference to the usual measure, namely the "market value," since there is only a very restricted true market for the shares and the price that would be likely to be realised as between a hypothetical willing buyer and seller would be significantly less than the value of the shares to their holder. At the root of the protection of minorities under Part XVII of the 1985 Act is the realisation of the value of shares held in non-quoted companies. The method of valuation is inevitably an artificial exercise.

CHAPTER 2

EQUITABLE EXCEPTIONS TO THE GENERAL PRINCIPLE OF MAJORITY RULE

Groups

2–001 A group of individuals will invariably have rules which contain the agreement of those individuals as to their respective rights as members of the group and as to the management of the affairs of the group. Those rules will usually provide that, in general, decisions of the group are to be arrived at by a simple majority vote of the members, who in turn agree to be bound by that majority decision. Such a provision has an obvious justification. The members have joined the group so as to benefit from their association with other individuals. In other words, each member calculates (or is deemed to calculate) that he can do better by belonging to a group than by acting on his own. The member cannot, however, have it both ways: he cannot require the minority to accept the majority decision when he is in the majority and then complain about the majority decision when he is in the minority.

In groups of any sophistication, however, the rules will protect certain members or certain classes of members (by definition a minority) from the will of the majority in certain circumstances. For example, the constitution of a sovereign state might provide that no citizen is to be discriminated against on the grounds of his race or religion, so that no decision of any majority, be it even a majority of all but one, could deprive an individual of such a right. There may be many variations of rules of this kind. The most obvious is the rule that makes provision for changing the rules. Thus, in the case of companies, it is usually provided that a three-quarters majority of members can change most rules. Certain rules, however, which exist for the protection of a particular class of member, may be made alterable only by a special majority vote of that class.

There will be certain rules, however, that can be broken with substantial impunity by a simple majority of members; for example, a rule may provide that not less than seven days' notice is required for any meeting of members. A particular meeting might be technically invalid because only six days' notice was given of it, but there is no point in the minority complaining about the majority decision because the result would have been the same even if an extra day's notice had been given. In other words, the breach of that rule could be regularised by convening a further meeting for the purpose of confirming what had occurred at the previous meeting.

2–002 Difficult questions of construction and interpretation may arise in respect of the rules of a group and, in particular, upon the implication of rights of members which cannot be overridden by a majority decision. There is one obvious limitation to the power of the majority, namely that any decision of the group can only extend to the affairs of the group and not to the personal affairs of the members. Furthermore, it might be fair, for example, to imply a rule that a member should not be expelled without good reason and fair compensation. Some groups might make express provision for expulsions, typically social clubs and trade unions. Similarly, it might also be fair to imply a rule that no majority should be entitled to appropriate to itself the group's property without good reason and fair compensation. The principal justification for the implication of each of these rules would be that, at the time of the making of the rules, nobody contemplated the possibility that any majority would act so unfairly and selfishly, and in a manner which was inconsistent with the spirit of association in a group. On the other hand, it could be argued that members were entitled to and invariably did vote in what they considered to be their own personal interests and there was never intended to be any guarantee against expulsion of a member. Clearly, much would depend on the type of group involved. In the case of a club formed for social or recreational purposes, membership would not be regarded as a thing of property or right. In the case of a trade union, membership would be regarded as a thing of value, even if not in the nature of alienable property. In the case of a small private trading company, membership would be regarded as property just like any other form of property, albeit subject to restrictions on alienation and, arguably, subject to the obligation to remain on good working relations with the other working members.

2–003 Particularly difficult questions of construction may arise in cases where some members, possibly a majority of members, have a personal interest in the issue to be decided by the group which, to a greater or lesser extent, appears to conflict with the interest of the group (whatever that might be). Generally speaking, it may be stated that such conflicts of interest should not disentitle the members with a conflict of interest from voting on the issue in question, since members are generally entitled to vote in their own personal interests, conflicts of interest will often arise, and who is to say what are the interests of the group with which the members' interests are said to be in conflict. For example, suppose a property-dealing company is proposing to buy a property in a neighbourhood in which a member lives. That member may be opposed to that purchase, not on commercial grounds but on the ground that the value of his home will be adversely affected by the proposed development. It might be argued that the interests and motives of that member should disentitle him from voting on the issue. There would, however, be enormous difficulties in proving that the member deliberately voted against the interests of the company, and the mere existence of the conflict of interest could not be sufficient, for otherwise members would be disenfranchised on numerous occasions. One can imagine the practical difficulties of policing a vote of members of a large public company with a view to excluding all those with a conflict of interest.

The moral pressure to disenfranchise members with a conflict of interest is particularly strong in cases where the members have in some way, and in some other capacity, wronged the group and the issue to be decided is whether the group should take legal proceedings against those members. That wrong may be of a fairly technical nature. For example, a member may be a shareholder of a company of which he is also a director. As director, he was under a strict fiduciary duty to account to the company for any profit he made as a result of his position as a director, even if the company itself could not have made that profit and could have had no objections to the profit made by the director. In such a case, where no harm has been done to the company, the argument in favour of disenfranchising the director from voting as a shareholder is weak. On the other hand, suppose the company had suffered loss as a result of the actions of the director. In such a case, the argument in favour of disenfranchisement would be stronger. Such a case would be analogous to the example, already given, of a majority appropriating to itself the group's property without good reason and fair compensation. On the face of it, the group would have every interest in pursuing the cause of action against the alleged wrongdoers and any opposition from the wrongdoers themselves is almost certainly motivated by interests contrary to those of the group.

2–004 On the assumption that the circumstances are such that certain members are disenfranchised because they have a conflict of interest, a procedural question then arises as to how the group can act at the instigation of the independent members. The rules of the group will almost certainly not have made provision for this eventuality. There will be pressure on the court to intervene and provide a remedy where none would otherwise exist. The court would have to choose between allowing any of the independent members to act on behalf of the group or allowing the court to convene a meeting of those whom it regards as independent members. In the latter case, the decision of that meeting would bind the group. This latter case appears to be preferable in principle. If a majority of independent shareholders make a particular decision, there can be no complaint made by the minority of independent shareholders. There may be very good reasons why it is not in the interests of a company, for example, to take proceedings against director/shareholders for wrongdoing. Private individuals contemplating litigation against third parties frequently decide not to pursue litigation which has good prospects of success, for any number of reasons. On the other hand, if the majority of independent shareholders object to the litigation in question on the ground of the costs involved and the risk of failure, then a minority shareholder might be willing to offer to shoulder the costs and the risks himself. Such an offer might be sufficient to persuade the majority or the court to permit the litigation to continue.

Companies

2–005 A company registered under the Companies Acts is a special type of group, but a group nevertheless. The principal difference between companies and most other groups is that a company is in law a separate person distinct from its members, whereas other groups (such as partnerships) are simply the sum of their members.

This distinctive feature of companies is insignificant in the limited sense that the company must act by its duly authorised organs, namely its board of directors and general meetings of members, and they are, respectively, collections of individuals. The separate legal personality of the company is, however, a crucial factor in limiting the number of occasions where a member can say that his personal rights, as opposed to the rights of the company, have been infringed. It is axiomatic that a wrong to the company is not necessarily a wrong to each member individually. If a minority shareholder wishes to escape from the general principle of majority rule, one of his routes will be to attempt to establish a personal wrong.[1]

2–006 The development of English law, in the field of the restrictions on the voting rights of shareholders in cases of conflict of interest and other circumstances, has proceeded on a case by case basis which virtually defies any attempt at rationalisation. Various attempts have been made in the authorities to state general principles, but none of them is really satisfactory. It is an extraordinary fact that this area of the law has never been directly considered by the House of Lords,[2] even though the 150th anniversary of the famous case of *Foss* v. *Harbottle*[3] will soon arrive. It is also remarkable that there has been room for significant advances in the last few years: see, for example, the litigation between Mr. Smith, Mr.

[1] See Chap. 5 below.
[2] But see the oblique relevance of *Regal (Hastings)* v. *Gulliver* [1942] 1 All E.R. 378.
[3] (1843) 2 Hare 461.

Croft and others.[4] Apart from the authorities dealing with the personal rights of shareholders, for example to enforce the rules of the company, the courts have applied general principles of equity and fairness, but narrowly and in a somewhat rigid and arbitrary fashion so as to preserve the obvious general principle of majority rule. To a large extent, these strivings towards a general equitable principle applicable to all cases of conflicts of interest on the part of a majority and oppression of minorities have been overtaken by the legislation referred to in Chapter 4 below, which is specifically addressed to the protection of minorities.[5] Nevertheless, the non-statutory limitations on the powers of a majority of shareholders remain of importance.

General Equitable Principles

2–007 It is submitted that the best way of analysing the authorities and of approaching any problem in practice in this area of the law is to answer two questions:

(1) Are the circumstances such that the votes of certain shareholders, because of their conflict of interest or for some other reason, should be disregarded on the issue in question?
(2) If certain votes are disregarded, is the decision of the majority of the remaining "good" votes binding?

2–008 As has already been indicated, the answer to the first question is, generally speaking, a resounding "no." In *Greenhalgh* v. *Arderne Cinemas*,[6] the articles of association of the company contained the common pre-emption provisions requiring members who wished to sell their shares to offer them first to existing members at their fair value. The majority shareholders concluded an agreement to sell their shares to a third party and then convened an extraordinary general meeting to amend the relevant article so as to add a proviso that it did not apply to transfers with the sanction of an ordinary resolution. The majority shareholders had a clear personal interest in securing the amendment: the amendment allowed them to complete their sale to the third party, and yet the minority shareholder continued to be prevented from doing likewise. The Court of Appeal did not even call on the majority shareholder for argument and, in a short judgment, unanimously held that the amendment was validly passed. Evershed M.R. referred to three well-known

[4] See [1988] Ch. 114.
[5] The development of the law in the context of the statutory remedy for unfair prejudice has been influenced by the authorities in the present context: compare *Re A Company (No. 00370 of 1987) ex p. Glossop* [1988] 1 W.L.R. 1068, 1075A with *Greenhalgh* v. *Arderne* (1951) Ch. 286, 291.
[6] [1951] Ch. 286.

cases dealing with expropriation of minority shareholders' interests in a company[7] and held:

> "Certain principles, I think, can be safely stated as emerging from those authorities. In the first place, I think it is now plain that 'bona fide for the benefit of the company as a whole' means not two things but one thing. It means that the shareholder must proceed upon what, in his honest opinion, is for the benefit of the company as a whole. The second thing is that the phrase, 'the company as a whole,' does not (at any rate in such a case as the present) mean the company as a commercial entity, distinct from the corporators: it means the corporators as a general body. That is to say, the case may be taken of an individual hypothetical member and it may be asked whether what is proposed is, in the honest opinion of those who voted in its favour, for that person's benefit. I think that the matter can, in practice, be more accurately and precisely stated by looking at the converse and by saying that a special resolution of this kind would be liable to be impeached if the effect of it were to discriminate between the majority shareholders and the minority shareholders, so as to give to the former an advantage of which the latter were deprived. When the cases are examined in which the resolution has been successfully attacked, it is on that ground. It is therefore not necessary to require that persons voting for a special resolution should, so to speak, dissociate themselves altogether from their own prospects and consider whether what is thought to be for the benefit of the company as a going concern. If, as commonly happens, an outside person makes an offer to buy all the shares, prima facie, if the corporators think it a fair offer and vote in favour of the resolution, it is no ground for impeaching the resolution that they are considering their own position as individuals."[8]

2–009 In theory, therefore, a minority shareholder can complain about a majority decision on two grounds:

(1) either the majority did not act bona fide for the benefit of the company; or
(2) the decision gave the majority an advantage that was denied to the minority.

As appears from the result of this case, however, it is apparent that, in practice, these limitations provide little protection for the minority. So far as concerns (1) and (2) above:

[7] *Sidebottom* v. *Kershaw, Leese & Co.* [1920] 1 Ch. 154; *Dafen Tinplate* v. *Llanelly Steel* [1920] 2 Ch. 124; and *Shuttleworth* v. *Cox* [1927] 2 K.B. 9.
[8] At p. 291.

(1) The onus of proof lies on the minority shareholder, and, unless the majority are ill-advised enough to disclose that they have disregarded the interests of the company, the facts must be so exceptional as to justify an inference that they have disregarded those interests.
(2) The decision must discriminate directly between shareholders and it is not sufficient that it confers an advantage on certain shareholders derived in practice from the fact of their being in the majority, since this is an advantage inherent in belonging to a majority.

In *Greenhalgh* v. *Arderne*, the minority shareholder was not prevented from selling his shares free from the pre-emption provisions: like any other shareholder, he required the consent of an ordinary resolution. The fact that, in reality, he would not obtain that consent whereas the majority would was insufficient.

2–010 The safeguards enunciated in *Greenhalgh* v. *Arderne* are not, however, completely toothless. In *Dafen Tinplate Co. Ltd.* v. *Llanelly Steel Co. (1907) Ltd.*[9] the articles of association of the company were altered to add a provision giving the member the right, by ordinary resolution, to require any shareholder to sell his shares to such person as was nominated by the board of directors and at a value declared by the board. The background to this alteration was that the majority shareholders did not approve of the action of a particular shareholder in transferring business to a competitor. Peterson J. held that, as a matter of fact, the alteration was not for the benefit of the company, and that the new article was too widely drawn and therefore permitted compulsory expropriation of a member's shares without justification.

2–011 In *Clemens* v. *Clemens Bros. Ltd.*[10] it was proposed to increase the company's issued share capital by issuing new shares to the directors and to an employees' trust. There were two existing shareholders, the plaintiff who held 45 per cent. of the shares and her aunt who held the balance. The plaintiff objected to the dilution of her shareholding, and in particular to the fact that she would hold less than 25 per cent. of the shares if the new issue proceeded. The facts were somewhat unusual, the aunt did not give evidence herself or call any evidence as to the reasons for the new issue, and Foster J. found as a fact that the proposed resolutions were "specifically and carefully designed to ensure that the plaintiff can never get control of the company but to deprive her of what has been called her negative control."[11]

[9] [1920] 2 Ch. 124.
[10] [1976] 2 All E.R. 268.
[11] At p. 282f–g.

The case of *Clemens* v. *Clemens* is, however, of interest for the observations made by the learned judge on *Greenhalgh* v. *Arderne*. The learned judge cited passages from the well-known cases of *Scottish Co-operative Wholesale Society Ltd.* v. *Meyer*[12] and *Re Westbourne Galleries*,[13] which were authorities on the statutory remedies under, respectively, sections 210 and 222(f) of the 1948 Act. He regarded the principles stated in these authorities as applicable to the general voting rights of majority shareholders, and concluded that such rights were "subject . . . to equitable considerations . . . which may make it unjust . . . to exercise [them] in a particular way."[14] It is respectfully submitted that this reasoning is unsound and that it was unnecessary, on the facts of the case, for the learned judge to extend the principles stated in *Greenhalgh* v. *Arderne* in the way that he did.

Derivative Actions

2–012 A common case of a shareholder appearing to act in his own interests rather than those of the company is one where it is alleged by a minority shareholder that the company has a cause of action against another shareholder which ought to be pursued by litigation. The principles stated in *Greenhalgh* v. *Arderne* are as applicable in this context as any other. Thus, if it can be positively shown that, at a meeting convened to consider the commencement of proceedings, certain shareholders did not exercise their votes bona fide for the benefit of the company, then their votes will be disregarded. There is, however, a logical conundrum inherent in a case such as this. In order to establish bad faith on the part of certain shareholders, another shareholder may wish to establish the claim of the company against them. The court, however, cannot allow that shareholder to establish that claim, because that would be contrary to the principle that only the company, and not every individual shareholder, can pursue a claim on its behalf. Furthermore, to disenfranchise every shareholder against whom it was alleged that a cause of action existed on behalf of the company would be contrary to the principles stated in *Greenhalgh* v. *Arderne*. The way in which the courts have attempted to resolve this conundrum is known, as a matter of legal jargon, as "the rule in *Foss* v. *Harbottle*" and the exceptions thereto. The rule comprehends the principle that an individual shareholder cannot initiate proceedings on behalf of the company, since that would be to drive a coach-and-horses through the principle of majority rule. It is said

[12] [1959] A.C. 324.
[13] [1973] A.C. 360.
[14] [1976] 2 All E.R. 268, 282d–e.

to be an exception to that rule if the circumstances justify the disenfranchisement of certain shareholders. Where a minority shareholder is allowed to bring proceedings on behalf of a minority shareholder, such proceeding are commonly called "derivative actions" in order to emphasise the fact that the plaintiff sues not on behalf of himself personally but on behalf of the company.

2–013 Although this issue will usually be something of a red herring, the right of a minority shareholder to bring a derivative action must, as a matter of strict logic, depend on showing that the decision to initiate proceedings on behalf of the company is vested in the shareholders in general meeting. If that decision is vested in the directors, then the votes of the shareholders will be irrelevant.

2–014 The question of whether the company ought to initiate and prosecute the necessary proceedings does not necessarily fall to be decided by the shareholders. Much will depend on the division of powers under the company's articles of association. Under articles of association in Table A form,[15] it has been held that the decision to bring proceedings on behalf of the company belongs to the board of directors as part of its general management powers, with which the members in general meeting are not entitled to interfere.[16] Thus, if the board of directors resolve to bring an action in the name of the company, there is nothing that the shareholders can do to stop the action, unless they remove the directors from office or it can be demonstrated that the directors have acted in breach of their fiduciary duties. Curiously, however, it is not clear from the authorities whether the shareholders can bring an action in the name of the company, if the board refuses or fails to do so. In *Marshall's Valve Gear Co. Ltd.* v. *Manning Wardle & Co. Ltd.*[17] it was held that the articles in that case, on their true construction, allowed the shareholders to bring an action whenever the directors declined to do so. It is submitted that the reasoning of this case can no longer be supported and Harman J. in *Breckland Group* v. *London and Suffolk Properties*[18] declined to follow it. In this recent case, an action was started in the name of the company by the majority shareholder against the managing director of the company. A shareholders' agreement provided that an action of this type could not be commenced without that managing director's consent. In an *ex tempore* judgment, Harman J. ordered a stay on the action to allow the board to consider whether to sanction the action. He rejected an

[15] See Regulation 80 of Table A (1948 form); Regulation 70 of Table A (1985 form).

[16] See *Automatic Self-Cleansing Filter Syndicate* v. *Cuninghame* [1906] 2 Ch. 34; *Shaw* v. *Shaw* [1935] 2 K.B. 113.

[17] [1909] 1 Ch. 267. See Gower's, *Principles of Modern Company Law* (4th ed.), pp. 147 and 643.

[18] [1989] B.C.L.C. 100.

argument that the shareholders could in any event sanction the action if the directors declined to do so.

2–015 If the power to initiate proceedings on behalf of the company belongs exclusively to the board of directors, which appears to be the case, it is superficially difficult to see on what basis a minority shareholder can bring a derivative action. Even if the board vote not to bring proceedings, and this vote is decided by the alleged wrongdoers themselves, on the face of it the minority shareholder (or, indeed, any of the shareholders) cannot complain since they are bound by the articles of association which vest such decisions in the board. This, however, is obviously too simplistic a view. If grounds exist to disenfranchise shareholders from voting on the matter, then clearly those same grounds will prevent those directors who are the same persons as the disenfranchised shareholders or who are associated with them from voting on the matter. If such grounds exist, since there is no basis for a derivative action sought by a minority director, the power to initiate proceedings on behalf of the company must vest, by default, in the shareholders.

2–016 The above inquiry as to the existence of the power of the member in general meeting to initiate proceedings on behalf of the company does, however, have some significance. There can be no justification for a derivative action if all the directors, or all those directors who choose to vote on the issue, are independent and untainted of any connection with the alleged wrongdoers. Furthermore, if the directors vote not to initiate proceedings, and the decision would have been the same even if the alleged wrongdoers and those associated with them had not voted, then that would be a strong reason not to permit a derivative action. In other words, if the majority of independent directors are against the initiation of proceedings, that must constitute such a reason. It may not, however, be decisive. The articles vested the board with certain powers to be exercised by the board as a whole. If certain of its members are disenfranchised, it is arguable that the voice of even the independent directors is not decisive.

2–017 It is now proposed to consider the leading authorities on the exceptions to the rule in *Foss* v. *Harbottle*, so far as those exceptions concern derivative actions. The following general propositions may be derived from these authorities, as follows:

2–018 (1) Cases are to be distinguished on the ground of the nature of the cause of action that is alleged to lie by the company against the shareholder or director in question. The authorities sometimes speak in terms of causes of action which are ratifiable by a majority of shareholders and those which are not. In the former cases, the alleged wrongdoers are not disenfranchised. In the latter cases, a minority shareholder is not necessarily bound by the decision of the majority. It is submitted that the above analysis in terms of ratifiability begs the question of whether the alleged wrongdoer is disenfranchised on a vote to initiate proceedings and is not of assistance.

(2) Having held that a given cause of action triggers the exception to the rule in *Foss* v. *Harbottle*, the court then disregards the votes of the alleged wrongdoers, without an investigation of the claim save to the extent that a prima facie case must be shown and without an investigation of their motives under the *Greenhalgh* v. *Arderne* test. In other words, the court does not generally[19] require, as a precondition to a derivative action, that it be positively shown that certain shareholders have not voted bona fide for the benefit of the company. **2–019**

(3) A derivative action will only be allowed where the alleged wrongdoers are in a position to defeat any proposed resolution of the shareholders that the company initiate proceedings against them.[20] In other words, if the majority of independent shareholders do not want to initiate proceedings, then a derivative action will not be allowed, since the decision not to initiate proceedings will have been reached even if the "tainted" votes are disregarded. The matter can be expressed in this way: if the "tainted" voters had abstained and the majority were still against the proceedings, then a minority shareholder could have no cause for complaint, and the minority shareholder cannot be in a better position because the "tainted" votes are exercised without any effect on the result. **2–020**

The Cause of Action Alleged

2–021 In *North-West Transportation Co. Ltd.* v. *Beatty*[21] a director contracted to sell a steamer to the company, and this contract required the assent of the members in general meeting. The director commanded a majority of votes and obtained that assent. All the independent shareholders opposed the resolution. The Privy Council held that the sale could not be set aside at the suit of a substantial independent shareholder. It was held that the director in question could vote on the issue despite his personal interest in the matter and that it was not shown that the sale was an improper one. Indeed, it was affirmatively proved that the sale was an entirely proper

[19] But see paras. 2–026 and 2–031.
[20] See paras. 2–027, etc.
[21] [1887] 12 App.Cas. 589. See also *Regal (Hastings)* v. *Gulliver* [1942] 1 All E.R. 378.

one.[22] Thus, far from it being in the interests of the company to rescind the sale, it would have been positively prejudicial to those interests to have done so. This case is a land-mark decision in establishing a shareholder's right to vote upon matters in which he has a personal interest. It also established that a cause of action by a company to set aside a sale made by a director to the company is not within the exceptions to the rule in *Foss* v. *Harbottle*, where all that is alleged is a conflict of interest on the part of the director in question and where it is not alleged that the sale was at an overvalue or otherwise prejudicial to the company.

2–022 By way of contrast, in *Cook* v. *Deeks*,[23] the controlling directors of the company diverted a contract to themselves in breach of trust and procured the passing of a resolution of the company in general meeting sanctioning their actions. The Privy Council held that a minority shareholder could bring an action to enforce the company's right to the contract in question. Lord Buckmaster L.C. held:

> "Even supposing it be not *ultra vires* of a company to make a present to its directors, it appears quite certain that directors holding a majority of votes would not be permitted to make a present to themselves. This would be to allow a majority to oppress the minority. To such cases the cases of *North-West Transportation* v. *Beatty* and *Burland* v. *Earle* have no application. . . . If their Lordships took the view that, in the circumstances of this case, the directors had exercised a discretion or decided on a matter of policy . . . different results would ensue, but this is not a conclusion which their Lordships are able to accept."[24]

Thus, if it is alleged that directors have caused loss to the company as a result of a breach of their fiduciary duty, then this will bring the case within the exceptions to the rule in *Foss* v. *Harbottle*.

2–023 The authorities in this area were considered in *Daniels* v. *Daniels*.[25] In that case, it was alleged that the controlling directors and majority shareholders had sold the company's land to one of them at an undervalue. Templeman J. refused an application by the directors to strike out the minority shareholder's action to set aside the sale. No allegation of actual fraud was made. It was held that:

[22] At p. 596.
[23] [1916] 1 A.C. 554.
[24] At pp. 564–565.
[25] [1978] Ch. 406.

> " . . . [A] minority shareholder who has no other remedy may sue where directors use their powers, intentionally or unintentionally, fraudulently or negligently, in a manner which benefits them at the expense of the company."[26]

2–024 The proposition that a controlling director, who makes a profit in breach of his fiduciary duties but not at the expense of the company, is not liable to a suit by a minority shareholder, is supported by dicta of the House of Lords in *Regal (Hastings)* v. *Gulliver.*[27]

In *Pavlides* v. *Jensen*[28] Danckwerts J. held that a minority shareholder could not bring an action for negligence against the controlling directors. This decision was distinguished by Templeman J. in *Daniels* v. *Daniels*, and by Vinelott J. in *Prudential Assurance* v. *Newman Industries (No. 2)*,[29] on the ground that the directors did not derive any personal benefit from their negligent actions. It is difficult, however, to see what difference it makes that no such personal benefit has been derived. The company has suffered loss, to the detriment of the general body of shareholders, and if the majority shareholders are to be relieved of an investigation of their liability for their loss, this is as much a case of the majority making off with the assets of the company as the facts of *Cook* v. *Deeks*. There is, therefore, a good argument that *Pavlides* v. *Jensen* was wrongly decided, and that the true test of whether the rule in *Foss* v. *Harbottle* applies to a particular cause of action is whether it is alleged that the company has suffered any loss.[30] Indeed, *Pavlides* v. *Jensen* could easily have been decided on the sounder ground that the majority of independent shareholders were against the initiation of proceedings against the directors.[31]

2–025 This approach is, it is submitted, supported by the decision of Megarry V.-C. in *Estmanco* v. *G.L.C.*[32] In that case, a local authority ("the council") had formed a company for the purpose of managing a block of flats. The council covenanted with the company to use its best endeavours to dispose of all the flats on long leases. The council then changed its policy and proposed to break that covenant. The shareholders of the company then consisted of the council, by a large majority, and 12 non-voting private shareholders who would have been prejudiced by the threatened breach of covenant. The council's case was as unmeritorious

[26] At p. 414D–E.
[27] [1942] 1 All E.R. 378.
[28] [1956] Ch. 565.
[29] [1981] Ch. 257 at p. 313D–E.
[30] *Pavlides* v. *Jensen* was, however, expressly approved by Dillon L.J. in *Multinational* v. *Multinational* [1983] Ch. 258, 289 B–E.
[31] The plaintiff in *Pavlides* v. *Jensen* was the holder of deferred shares who had no right to attend or vote at general meetings.
[32] [1982] 1 W.L.R. 2.

as was that of the directors in *Pavlides* v. *Jensen*. Megarry V.-C. held that one of the private shareholders could bring a derivative action to enforce the terms of the covenant against the council. In a wide-ranging judgment, Megarry V.-C. rejected the council's argument that it had acted in what it believed to be in the best interests of the company:

> "Now the question is how far authorities such as these[33] on the validity of making alterations in the articles fit in with the rule in *Foss* v. *Harbottle* and its exceptions; for Mr. Brodie [counsel for the council] accepted, as he had to, that the line of authority on altering the articles has not yet been applied to the rule in *Foss* v. *Harbottle* and its exceptions. I do not think that Mr. Brodie ever succeeded in answering that question satisfactorily. Plainly there must be some limit to the power of the majority to pass resolutions which they believe to be in the best interests of the company and yet remain immune from interference by the courts. It may be in the best interests of the company to deprive the minority of some of their rights or some of their property, yet I do not think that this gives the majority an unrestricted right to do this, however unjust it may be, and however much it may harm shareholders whose rights as a class differ from those of the majority. If a case falls within one of the exceptions from *Foss* v. *Harbottle*, I cannot see why the right of the minority to sue under that exception should be taken away from them merely because the majority of the company reasonably believe it to be in the best interests of the company that this should be done."[34]

The learned judge then referred to *Daniels* v. *Daniels* and observed:

> "Apart from the benefit to themselves at the company's expense, the essence of the matter seems to be an abuse or misuse of power. 'Fraud' in the phrase 'fraud on a minority' seems to be being used as comprising not only fraud at common law but also fraud in the wider equitable sense of that term, as in the equitable concept of a fraud on a power."[35]

On the facts, he then held as follows:

> "There can be no doubt about the 12 voteless purchasers being a minority; there can be no doubt about the advantage to the council of having the action discontinued; there can be no doubt about the injury to the applicant and the rest of the minority, both as shareholders and as purchasers, of that discontinuance; and I feel

[33] *e.g. Greenhalgh* v. *Arderne (supra.)*
[34] At pp. 11G–12B.
[35] At p. 12F–G.

little doubt that the council has used its voting power not in order to promote the best interests of the company but in order to bring advantage to itself and disadvantage to the minority. Furthermore, that disadvantage is no trivial matter, but represents a radical alteration in the basis on which the council sold the flats to the minority. It seems to me that the sum total represents a fraud on the minority in the sense in which 'fraud' is used in that phrase, or alternatively represents such an abuse of power as to have the same effect."[36]

This decision is of interest, since it appears to involve an actual finding that the council had acted contrary to the principles stated in *Greenhalgh* v. *Arderne*, but at an interlocutory hearing and without any oral evidence on this issue. It should be noted that this decision was made before that of the Court of Appeal in *Prudential* v. *Newman Industries (No. 2)*,[37] which is discussed below. It is arguable that Megarry V.-C. need not have gone as far as deciding actual abuse of power on the part of the council: he need only have decided that there was a prima facie cause of action which the independent shareholders wished to pursue. But this decision may point to the existence of cases where a court is prepared at an interlocutory hearing to find actual abuse of power on the part of the defendants in stifling the proceedings against them, without investigating the merits of the action against them. A court might, for example, adopt this approach where the cause of action was one of negligence and, therefore, be able to distinguish *Pavlides* v. *Jensen*. In other words, the potential defendants would not be automatically disenfranchised as shareholders, but their reasons, and those of the independent shareholders, would be closely scrutinised. **2–026**

Control

The facts of *Prudential* v. *Newman Industries*[38] were unusual in that they concerned the affairs of a public quoted company, whose shares were widely held by institutional and private investors and whose board of directors consisted of executive directors (some of whom were the defendants) and independent non-executive directors. The allegations made by the minority shareholder, which was an institutional investor with a 3.2 per cent. shareholding in the company, against two of the executive directors ("the defendants") were pleaded very broadly, for instance the sending of "tricky" and "misleading" circulars to shareholders, but were essentially that the company had been induced by their **2–027**

[36] At pp. 15H–16B.
[37] [1982] Ch. 204.
[38] [1981] Ch. 25; revsd. [1982] Ch. 204. The principal individual defendant, Mr. Bartlett, wrote a book about the case: *Power, Prejudice and Pride* (1982).

fraud to buy assets from another company ("T.P.G.") at an overvalue. T.P.G. held 25 per cent. of the company's shares. The defendants controlled 35 per cent. of T.P.G.'s shares. Before the action was heard, one of the defendants resigned as a director of the company. Upon application by the company and the defendants to strike out the action, Vinelott J. declined to decide, as a preliminary issue, whether the plaintiff had established the requisite degree of control by the defendants of the company's affairs.[39] Having heard the evidence, he found in favour of the plaintiff. The defendants appealed, but the company then indicated that it would take advantage of an order made against the defendants despite its previous opposition to the proceedings. The Court of Appeal held that, because of this indication, it was too late to consider whether the plaintiff had established the requisite degree of control. They did, however, make certain trenchant observations on the proper approach to take to an application to strike out derivative action:

> "In the result it would be improper for us to express any concluded view on the proper scope of the exception or exceptions to the rule in *Foss* v. *Harbottle*. We desire, however, to say two things. First, as we have already said, we have no doubt whatever that Vinelott J. erred in dismissing the summons of May 10, 1979 [to strike out]. He ought to have determined as a preliminary issue whether the plaintiffs were entitled to sue on behalf of Newman by bringing a derivative action. It cannot have been right to have subjected the company to a 30-day action (as it was then estimated to be) in order to enable him to decide whether the plaintiffs were entitled in law to subject the company to a 30-day action. Such an approach defeats the whole purpose of the rule in *Foss* v. *Harbottle* and sanctions the very mischief that the rule is designed to prevent. By the time a derivative action is concluded, the rule in *Foss* v. *Harbottle* can have little, if any, role to play. Either the wrong is proved, thereby establishing conclusively the rights of the company; or the wrong is not proved, so *cadit quaestio*. In the present case a board, of which all the directors save one were disinterested, with the benefit of the [independent] Schroder-Harman report, had reached the conclusion before the start of the action that the prosecution of the action was likely to do more harm than good. That might prove a sound or unsound assessment, but it was the commercial assessment of an apparently independent board. Obviously the board would not have expected at that stage to be as well informed about the affairs of the company as it might be after 36 days of evidence in court and an intense examination of some 60 files of documents. But the board clearly doubted whether there were sufficient reasons for supposing

[39] [1981] Ch. 25.

that the company would at the end of the day be in a position to count its blessings; and clearly feared, as counsel said, that it might be killed by kindness. Whether in the events which have happened Newman (more exactly the disinterested body of shareholders) will feel that it has all been well worth while, or must lick its wounds and render no thanks to those who have interfered in its affairs, is not a question which we can answer. But we think it is within the bounds of possibility that if the preliminary issue had been argued, a judge might have reached the considered view that prosecution of this great action should be left to the decision of the board or of a specially convened meeting of the shareholders, albeit less well informed than a judge after a 72-day action.

So much for the summons of May 10. The second observation which we wish to make is merely a comment on Vinelott J.'s decision that there is an exception to the rule in *Foss* v. *Harbottle* whenever the justice of the case so requires. We are not convinced that this is a practical test, particularly if it involves a full-dress trial before the test is applied. On the other hand we do not think that the right to bring a derivative action should be decided as a preliminary issue upon the hypothesis that all the allegations in the statement of claim of 'fraud' and 'control' are facts, as they would be on the trial of a preliminary point of law. In our view, whatever may be the properly defined boundaries of the exception to the rule, the plaintiff ought at least to be required before proceeding with his action to establish a prima facie case (i) that the company is entitled to the relief claimed, and (ii) that the action falls within the proper boundaries of the exception to the rule in *Foss* v. *Harbottle*. On the latter issue it may well be right for the judge trying the preliminary issue to grant a sufficient adjournment to enable a meeting of shareholders to be convened by the board, so that he can reach a conclusion in the light of the conduct of, and proceedings at, that meeting."[40]

2–028 The above observations leave the following questions unresolved:

(1) Who is an independent shareholder or director for these purposes?
(2) Who is to be consulted: the independent directors or the independent shareholders or both?
(3) Is the decision of those consulted binding on the court? If not, what other considerations does the court take into account?

It seems to follow from those observations that the court can consult either the independent shareholders or the independent directors or both of them, and that the court is not bound by their decision.

[40] [1982] Ch. 204, 221A–222B.

2–029 The above issues subsequently fell to be considered in *Smith* v. *Croft (No. 2)*.[41] In that case Knox J. held that a preliminary issue should be tried as to whether the plaintiff had established a prima facie cause of action by the company against the defendants and whether the action was within the exception to the rule in *Foss* v. *Harbottle*. The facts of the case were as follows. There was a prima facie case that the defendant directors had caused the company to make certain illegal and *ultra vires* payments. There was no doubt that the defendants controlled the majority of votes at board level. The position at general meeting level was more complicated. The defendants controlled about 65 per cent. of the shares. The plaintiffs held about 12 per cent. of the shares and had the support of another shareholder with about 2.5 per cent. of the shares. The remaining approximately 20 per cent. of the shares were held by another company ("Wren"). Wren had indicated that it opposed the plaintiffs' action.

2–030 It is important to note that *Smith* v. *Croft (No. 2)* was concerned with an allegedly *ultra vires* transaction, and it was clear on the authorities[42] that it was not necessary to show that the defendants by reason of their control of the company were able to prevent the bringing of proceedings. Knox J., however, clearly regarded a minority shareholder's action to correct (as opposed to prevent) an *ultra vires* transaction as no different from an action such as that in *Cook* v. *Deeks*. Knox J. held:

> "As to that Mr. Potts [counsel for the plaintiff] submitted that no reported authority held that in a case falling within the fraud on a minority exception to the rule in *Foss* v. *Harbottle* the court should go beyond seeing whether the wrongdoers are in control and count heads to see what the other shareholders; *i.e.* those other than the plaintiffs and the wrongdoers, think should be done. I accept that in many reported cases the court has not gone on to the second stage. *Mason* v. *Harris* (1879) 11 Ch.D. 97 is one such case, and there are modern examples too, such as *Pavlides* v. *Jensen* [1956] Ch. 565 and *Daniels* v. *Daniels* [1978] Ch. 406. But the fact that such an investigation was not conducted is not conclusive that it could not be conducted, more especially in the absence of any argument on this precise point. An investigation for interlocutory purposes of the propriety of the exercise of voting power in connection with the proposed prosecution of a minority shareholder's action was conducted by Sir Robert Megarry V.-C. in *Estmanco (Kilner House) Ltd.* v. *Greater London Council* [1982] 1 W.L.R. 2. In that case he permitted the action to proceed, but Mr. Aldous [counsel for the defendants] submitted that the careful scrutiny to which the propriety

[41] [1988] Ch. 114.
[42] See at pp. 173–177.

of the shareholders' voting activities was subjected is of itself an indication of the significance that the court in a proper case will attach to it. This I accept.

'. . .'

In my judgment the word 'control' was deliberately placed in inverted commas by the Court of Appeal in *Prudential Assurance Co. Ltd.* v. *Newman Industries Ltd. (No. 2)* [1982] Ch. 204, 219 because it was recognised that voting control by the defendants was not necessarily the sole subject of investigation. Ultimately the question which has to be answered in order to determine whether the rule in *Foss* v. *Harbottle* applies to prevent a minority shareholder seeking relief as plaintiff for the benefit of the company is 'Is the plaintiff being improperly prevented from bringing these proceedings on behalf of the company?' If it is an expression of the corporate will of the company by an appropriate independent organ that is preventing the plaintiff from prosecuting the action he is not improperly but properly prevented and so the answer to the question is 'No.' The appropriate independent organ will vary according to the constitution of the company concerned and the identity of the defendants who will in most cases be disqualified from participating by voting in expressing the corporate will.

Finally on this aspect of the matter I remain unconvinced that a just result is achieved by a single minority shareholder having the right to involve a company in an action for recovery of compensation for the company if all the other minority shareholders are for disinterested reasons satisfied that the proceedings will be productive of more harm than good. If Mr. Potts' argument is well founded once control by the defendants is established the views of the rest of the minority as to the advisability of the prosecution of the suit are necessarily irrelevant. I find that hard to square with the concept of a form of pleading originally introduced on the ground of necessity alone in order to prevent a wrong going without redress."[43]

2–031 It is, therefore, submitted that the decision in *Smith* v. *Croft (No. 2)* is as applicable to a cause of action as pursued in *Cook* v. *Deeks* as any other cause of action pursued by a shareholder on behalf of the company.

Knox J. held that, on the basis that the independent shareholders should be consulted, the relevant test of independence was as follows:

"In my judgment in this case votes should be disregarded if, but only if, the court is satisfied either that the vote or its equivalent is actually cast with a view to supporting the defendants rather than securing benefit to the company, or that the situation of the person whose vote is considered is such that there is a substantial risk of that happening. The court should not substitute its own opinion but can,

[43] At pp. 184C–F, 184H–185E.

and in my view should, assess whether the decision making process is vitiated by being or being likely to be directed to an improper purpose."[44]

Applying that test the learned judge concluded:

> "(T)here is no sufficient evidence that in relation to the present question whether these proceedings should continue Wren Trust has reached its conclusion on any grounds other than reasons genuinely thought to advance the company's interests. It is not for me to say whether the decision itself is right or wrong. It is for me to say whether the process by which it was reached can be impugned and I hold that it cannot. Nor do I consider that in the circumstances there is shown to have been a substantial risk of Wren Trust's vote having been cast in order to support the defendants as opposed to securing the benefit of the company."[45]

2–032 It was clear that Wren would vote against the continuation of the action. Without further ado, the learned judge struck out the plaintiff's action.[46] In other words, he regarded the decision of the majority of independent shareholders as determinative of the issue. On the face of the decision of the Court of Appeal in *Prudential* v. *Newman Industries (No. 2)*, the court retains a discretion to override the decision of the majority of independent shareholders. It is difficult, however, to conceive of circumstances where this would occur. It would be a brave court which allowed a minority shareholder's action to continue despite the opposition of independent directors or shareholders in the light of the Court of Appeal's comments in *Prudential* v. *Newman Industries (No. 2)*.

2–033 It is submitted that the court must have a discretion[47] whether to consult the independent directors in addition to the independent shareholders. In principle, if there is a substantial number of independent directors, then their views should carry considerable weight, since management powers will probably have been delegated to them under the articles of association. The court would, no doubt, however, take into consideration the number of the independent directors, their reasons for their decision, their shareholdings in the company, and weigh those against the number of independent shareholders and their decision. There is no limit to the number of possible permutations. If no clear consensus amongst independent directors and shareholders could be discerned, the

[44] At p. 186D–F.
[45] At p. 189C–E.
[46] See also *Taylor* v. *N.U.M.* [1985] B.C.L.C. 237, 254–255.
[47] It is implicit in the Court of Appeal's judgment in *Prudential* v. *Newman Industries (No. 2)* that the views of the independent directors were important.

court might allow the action to continue, on the basis that the plaintiff continued it at his own risk as to costs.

2–034 The point that a minority shareholder cannot bring an action on behalf of the company unless he is unjustly prevented from doing so by the majority is illustrated by the case of a company in liquidation. In such a case, it is the liquidator, if necessary with the sanction of the liquidation committee or the court, who has the power to initiate proceedings on behalf of the company: neither the directors nor the shareholders have that power after the company has gone into liquidation. There can, therefore, be no question of the majority shareholders stifling an action on behalf of the company, so there can be no grounds for a minority shareholder's action.[48] A shareholder may, however, apply to the court for leave to bring an action in the name of the company, or to bring proceedings for misfeasance against former directors.[49]

Procedure

2–035 It is well established that the form of a minority shareholder's action is one in which the shareholder is the plaintiff suing on behalf of himself and all other shareholders other than the defendants, and that the company must be joined as a defendant.

2–036 As appears from the passage in the judgment of the Court of Appeal in *Prudential* v. *Newman Industries (No. 2)* cited at paragraph 2–027 above, the defendants are entitled to have determined as a preliminary issue whether the plaintiff has established:

> "a prima facie case
> (i) that the company is entitled to the relief claimed, and
> (ii) that the action falls within the proper boundaries of the exception to the rule in *Foss* v. *Harbottle*."

A minority shareholder would, therefore, be well advised, before commencing proceedings, to assemble his evidence in support of the action against the defendants, and to invite the board and a meeting of shareholders to consider initiating an action on the basis of that evidence. The potential defendants, if they were well advised, would then either answer those allegations or commission an independent report on them, and then attempt to persuade meetings of the independent directors and shareholders that it would not be worthwhile litigating the matter.

[48] See *Ferguson* v. *Wallbridge* [1935] 3 D.L.R. 66; *Fargro* v. *Godfrey* [1986] 1 W.L.R. 1134.
[49] See s. 212(5) of the Insolvency Act 1986.

Costs

2–037 One important factor to be considered by an independent director or shareholder would be the incidence of costs in the proposed litigation. Since the minority shareholder would be suing on behalf of the company and all shareholders and not on behalf of himself alone, he would prima facie be entitled to an indemnity as to costs from the company if the action were successful. Indeed, even if the action were unsuccessful but the court took the view that the plaintiff had acted reasonably in bringing the action, the court might give him such an indemnity.[50]

By analogy with the procedure whereby a trustee can apply for an indemnity from a beneficiary on whose behalf he is suing,[51] a procedure has grown up whereby a minority shareholder can apply to the court at an interlocutory stage for an order that the company do indemnify him as to the costs of the action.[52] Buckley L.J. contemplated that such an application would take the following form:

> "After issuing his writ a minority shareholder plaintiff could apply by summons in the action for directions as to whether he should proceed in the action and, if so, to what stage without further directions. I think that such an application should in the first instance be made *ex parte*. In a relatively simple case the court may feel able to deal with the matter without joinder of any other party. When the summons comes before the court, directions could be given as to whether the company or another minority shareholder or the defendants or any of them or anyone else should be made respondents and whether any respondent should be appointed to act in a representative capacity for the purposes of the summons. The court might at this stage think it desirable to require the plaintiff to circularise or convene a meeting of other minority shareholders and to place their views, so far as ascertained, before the court. The summons should be supported by affidavit evidence of any relevant facts, to which instructions to counsel and his opinion thereon should be exhibited. The respondent or respondents to the summons, if any, would also be permitted to file evidence. The evidence of other parties would not be disclosed to the defendants in the action unless the court so directed and the defendants, if made respondents to the summons, would not be permitted to be present when the merits of the application were discussed. Upon the effective hearing of the summons the court would determine whether the plaintiff should be authorised to proceed with the action and, if so, to what stage he should be

[50] See *per* Buckley L.J. in *Wallersteiner* v. *Moir (No. 2)* [1975] Q.B. 373, 404. But see now *Smith* v. *Croft (No. 2),* note 41 above.
[51] *Re Beddoe* [1893] 1 Ch. 547.
[52] *Wallersteiner* v. *Moir (No. 2)* [1975] Q.B. 373.

> authorised to do so without further directions from the court. The plaintiff, acting under the authority of such a direction, would be secure in the knowledge that, when the costs of the action should come to be dealt with, this would be upon the basis, as between himself and the company, that he has acted reasonably and ought prima facie to be treated by the trial judge as entitled to an order that the company should pay his costs, which should, I think, normally be taxed on a basis not less favourable than the common fund basis, and should indemnify him against any costs he may be ordered to pay to the defendants. Should the court not think fit to authorise the plaintiff to proceed, he would do so at his own risk as the costs.."[53]

2–038 In *Jaybird Group* v. *Greenwood*,[54] a case decided very soon after the Court of Appeal judgment in *Prudential* v. *Newman Industries (No. 2)* but not apparently with the benefit of sight of that judgment, the court held, in the light of evidence filed but not seen by the defendants but upon hearing submissions on their behalf, that the action was one which would have been commenced by an independent board of the company. Accordingly, the plaintiff was given an order for the indemnity down to discovery and inspection. The learned judge held that the plaintiff did not have to establish that he was impecunious.

2–039 In *Smith* v. *Croft (No. 1)*,[55] which was the same action as that in *Smith* v. *Croft (No. 2)* referred to above, the plaintiff had applied for an order of indemnity from the company. Walton J. held that the usual procedure should be that the applicant applied on notice. Furthermore, the defendants should see all relevant evidence, except for that protected by legal professional privilege or that which if disclosed "would stultify the success of the action."[56] The learned judge gave the following examples of the latter type of documents: those which would disclose the identity of a "mole" in the company, or which tended to show that the defendants were trying to cover their tracks. In refusing to make an order for an indemnity, the learned judge applied the following test:

> "The standard suggested by Buckley L.J. [in *Wallersteiner* v. *Moir (No. 2)*] was that of an independent board of directors exercising the standard of care which prudent businessmen would exercise in their own affairs. Would such an independent board consider that it ought to bring the action?"[57]

[53] At pp. 404E–405C.
[54] [1986] B.C.L.C. 319.
[55] [1986] 2 All E.R. 551; [1986] 1 W.L.R. 580.
[56] At p. 558h.
[57] At p. 559j.

Personal Rights of Shareholders

2–040 In *Edwards* v. *Halliwell*[58] Jenkins L.J., in a well-known judgment, observed that, in addition to the cases of "fraud on the minority" which have been discussed in the preceding section, there were other classes of cases which were exceptions to the rule in *Foss* v. *Harbottle*.[59]

The ambit of these "exceptions," and their relationship to the wider question of the personal rights of shareholders as distinct from the rights of the company, are discussed in Chapter 5 below.

The Unfair Prejudice Remedy

2–041 Under section 461 of the 1985 Act, where the court is satisfied that the affairs of a company have been conducted in a manner unfairly prejudicial to some parts of its members, it may direct that the prejudiced minority shall have the power to bring a derivative action. In theory, therefore, a minority shareholder need not proceed immediately to a derivative action but could apply first for leave to do so on the unfair prejudice ground. It is not clear in what circumstances a court would give such leave where the circumstances would not otherwise have justified a derivative action. This is an area that has yet to be explored by the courts.

Miscellaneous

2–042 Two further points should be noted in respect of a derivative action brought by a minority shareholder:

(1) In cases of the majority shareholders stifling a cause of action of the company against them, it is not necessary that the minority shareholder should have been a shareholder at the time that the cause of action accrued.[60] It appears, however, that he must be registered as a member at the time of the commencement of the action.[61]

(2) Since the court is granting the minority shareholder an indulgence in equity to bring an action in the name of the company, the minority shareholder must come with "clean hands," and the court may have regard to all the circumstances in deciding whether it is just to allow the derivative action.[62]

[58] [1950] 2 All E.R. 1064.
[59] At pp. 1066–1069. See [1982] Ch. 204, 210.
[60] *Seaton* v. *Grant* [1867] L.R. 2 Ch.App. 459.
[61] *Birch* v. *Sullivan* [1957] 1 W.L.R. 1247. This may not be an absolute rule.
[62] See, for example, *Nurcombe* v. *Nurcombe* [1985] 1 W.L.R. 370.

Conclusion

2–043 It is submitted that a common theme is present in all the authorities discussed in this chapter, from *Greenhalgh* v. *Arderne* through to *Smith* v. *Croft (No. 2)*, namely that the court will intervene to protect the minority from the majority decision where the majority's actions or omissions are unconscionable. Such circumstances are sometimes expressed as a "fraud on the minority," and the court's right to intervene is sometimes based on the equitable doctrine of "fraud on a power."[63] The law has achieved a certain degree of predictability and sophistication in the context of derivative actions against allegedly wrongdoing directors or shareholders. In other contexts, however, such as the facts of *Greenhalgh* v. *Arderne*, the minority was granted protection only in the most exceptional circumstances. The supposed limitation on the power of the majority, namely that it must act bona fide for the benefit of the company, as enunciated in *Greenhalgh* v. *Arderne* can be seen either as an unrealistic and impractical limitation or as an implied statement that nothing short of actual bad faith will suffice to justify intervention by the court.[64] An unsatisfactory attempt was made in *Clemens* v. *Clemens* to interpret *Greenhalgh* v. *Arderne* in a liberal fashion. Judge-made law was then overtaken by, first, section 210 of the 1948 Act and, then, section 75 of the Companies Act 1980 ("the 1980 Act"), now section 459 of the 1985 Act.

[63] *e.g. Estmanco* v. *G.L.C.* (*supra*).

[64] For circumstances where the court held that the majority had acted unjustly although bona fide for the benefit of the company, see *Re Westbourne Galleries* discussed in Chap. 3, paras. 3–015, etc.

Chapter 3

WINDING-UP ON THE JUST AND EQUITABLE GROUND

Section 122(1)(g) of the Insolvency Act 1986 ("the 1986 Act") provides: **3–001**

"(1) a company may be wound up by the court if—

(g) the court is of the opinion that it is just and equitable that the company should be wound up."

Section 125(2) of the 1986 Act adds as follows:

"(2) If the petition is presented by members of the company on the ground that it is just and equitable that the company should be wound up, the court, if it is of opinion—

(a) that the petitioners are entitled to relief either by winding up the company or by some other means, and

(b) that in the absence of any other remedy it would be just and equitable that the company should be wound up,

shall make a winding-up order; but this does not apply if the court is also of the opinion both that some other remedy is available to the petitioners and that they are acting unreasonably in seeking to have the company wound up instead of pursuing that other remedy."

The courts have, however, placed little reliance upon section 125(2) of the 1986 Act, other than in the context of offers to buy the petitioner's shares at a value to be determined by an accountant. These issues are discussed further at paragraph 3–031 below. **3–002**

Locus Standi

Section 124(2) of the 1986 Act provides: **3–003**

"(2) Except as mentioned below, a contributory[1] is not entitled to present a winding-up petition unless either—

[1] A contributory is defined as a "person liable to contribute to the assets of a company in the event of its being wound up": s. 79(1) of the 1986 Act.

(a) the number of members is reduced below 2, or
(b) the shares in respect of which he is a contributory, or some of them, either were originally allotted to him, or have been held by him, and registered in his name, for at least six months during the 18 months before the commencement of the winding up, or have devolved on him through the death of a former holder."

3–004 Whether a proposed petitioner is or is not a contributory of the company within the meaning of sections 76 to 82 of the 1986 Act is unlikely to be of any significance, save in those rare cases falling within section 124(2)(a) of the 1986 Act.[2] The principal *locus standi* requirement is that the proposed petitioner's shares either:

(1) were originally allotted to him, or
(2) have been held by him and registered in his name for at least six months during the 18 months before the presentation of the petition.[3]

Theoretically the proposed petitioner does not have to be registered as a member at the time of presentation of the petition: he could, for example, be a past member,[4] but the circumstances must be very rare for a past member to have grounds to present a winding-up petition.

3–005 Therefore, apart from original allottees of shares, it is usually vital that the proposed petitioner be registered as a member in the books of the company, and has been so registered for at least 6 months, at the time of presentation of the petition. Thus, if a proposed petitioner claims that he has been wrongly omitted from the company's register of members, he will have to obtain an order for rectification of the register under section 359 of the 1985 Act and then wait six months before he can present a winding-up petition.

3–006 So far as concerns original allottees of shares, it is not essential that they be registered as members or have held their shares for any period.[5] Section 738(1) of the 1985 Act provides that " . . . shares are to be taken for the purposes of this Act to be allotted when a person acquires the unconditional right to be included in the company's register of members

[2] The significance of a company having less than two members is that the remaining shareholder is personally liable for its debts: s. 24 of the 1985 Act; s. 122(e) of the 1986 Act.
[3] See s. 129(1) of the 1986 Act.
[4] Provided he is a "contributory."
[5] See *Re JN2 Ltd.* [1977] 3 All E.R. 1104.

in respect of those shares." In *Re A Company (No. 003160 of 1986)*[6] it was alleged that shares were originally allotted to the co-petitioner's wife as nominee for the co-petitioner. Hoffmann J. held that the co-petitioner had no *locus standi* to present a winding-up petition, since under the alleged agreement it was provided that the co-petitioner's wife should be registered as a member, not the co-petitioner.

3–007 Even if the proposed petitioner has been registered as a member of the company for the requisite period, it is the practice of the court to strike the petition out if there is a bona fide and substantial dispute about the petitioner's entitlement to be so registered. The same principle applies in the case of a dispute about an original allottee's entitlement to be registered as a shareholder. In *Re JN2 Ltd.*,[7] a case involving an original allottee, Brightman J. held that, by analogy with the practice in winding-up petitions presented by creditors of a company, the dispute between two persons as to entitlement to be registered as a shareholder should be determined before presentation of a winding-up petition, because of the serious consequences of such a petition for a trading company.[8]

3–008 The above-mentioned practice of the court in the case of disputes over shares is not invariably applied. In *Re Garage Door Associates Ltd.*[8a] the petitioner ("G") was registered as the holder of one share and presented a petition, seeking relief on the unfair prejudice ground and for winding-up in the alternative, in which he challenged the validity of an issue of 799 shares to other shareholders. The other shareholders had already presented a petition against G, seeking relief on the unfair prejudice ground, in which they alleged that the one share registered in G's name was held on trust for them. Mervyn Davies J. held that the issues as to share ownership could be determined in the course of the petitions.[9]

Tangible Interest

3–009 It is but common sense that a shareholder should not be permitted to petition to wind up a company if he will gain nothing from a winding-up. In general, therefore, if the company is insolvent, in the sense that there will be no surplus for shareholders after payment of the company's debts and the costs and expenses of the liquidation, then a fully paid-up shareholder's petition will be struck out. Indeed, any shareholder's

[6] [1986] B.C.L.C. 391.
[7] See n. 5 above.
[8–8a] See *Re Garage Door Associates Ltd.* [1984] 1 W.L.R. 35. See also *Re Claybridge Shipping* [1981] Comm. L.R. 107, for comments by the Court of Appeal on the practice in the case of disputed creditors' petitions. The practice is not inflexible.
[9] See also *Re A Company (No. 001363 of 1988)* (1989) 5 B.C.C. 18.

petition which does not expressly plead such a surplus is liable to be struck out.[10] In the normal case, therefore, the petitioner must allege a surplus and then, at trial, prove that surplus, which is not merely negligible,[11] on a balance of probabilities.[12] If the company alleges that it is insolvent and seeks to strike out the petition *in limine*, it will have to show that the petitioner's allegation of surplus is "obviously unsustainable."[13]

3–010 There is one clear exception to this general rule, namely where " . . . the petitioner's inability to prove his tangible interest is due to the company's own default in providing him with information to which as a member he is entitled."[14] This exception is limited in scope, since a member has only a limited right to information from the company. For example, he has no right to inspect the minute book of the board and he has no right to see financial information made available to the management: his sole right is to receive audited accounts in accordance with the 1985 Act.

3–011 Another, although unusual, exception is the case of a single shareholder seeking the winding-up of a company with only one shareholder: see sections 122(e) and 124(2)(a) of the 1986 Act, and section 24 of the 1985 Act. The same observations would apply to a shareholder of an unlimited company.

3–012 In theory, a shareholder might be able to show some tangible interest in a winding-up even though there would not be a surplus. In *Re Chesterfield Catering Co. Ltd.*[15] Oliver J. cited Jessel M.R.'s reference to "a sufficient interest to entitle him to ask for the winding up of the company" in *Re Rica Gold Washing Co. Ltd.*[16] and held:

> "However, it is I think clear that in referring to 'a sufficient interest' Jessel M.R. meant an interest by virtue of the petitioner's membership. In order to establish his *locus standi* to petition a fully paid shareholder must, as it seems to me, show that he will, as a member of the company, achieve some advantage, or avoid or minimise some disadvantage, which would accrue to him by virtue of his membership of the company. For instance, a member of a company might have a strong interest in terminating its life because he was engaged in a competing business or because he was engaged in litigation with

[10] *Re Rica Gold Washing Co. Ltd.* (1879) 11 Ch.D. 36.
[11] See *Re Martin Coulter* [1988] B.C.L.C. 12, 17c.
[12] *Re Expanded Plugs Ltd.* [1966] 1 W.L.R. 514.
[13] See *Re Martin Coulter* [1988] B.C.L.C. 12, 18.
[14] *Per* Hoffmann J. in *Re Commercial and Industrial Insulations Ltd.* [1986] B.C.L.C. 191.
[15] [1977] Ch. 373.
[16] See n. 10 above.

the company, but I do not think that that was the sort of interest that Jessel M.R. had in mind."[17]

3–013 It is submitted, however, that in the case of a fully paid-up shareholder of a limited company it is very difficult to conceive of any "sufficient interest" other than an interest in a surplus on winding-up.

Just and Equitable

3–014 There is no limit to the range of circumstances which may justify a winding-up order on the just and equitable ground, nor is there any great advantage in attempting to classify those circumstances. The three most common types of circumstances may, however, be stated as:

(1) Expulsion from office.
(2) Loss of confidence in management.
(3) Deadlock in the management of the affairs of the company.

(1) *Expulsion from office*[18]

3–015 This class of cases is, arguably, the most far-reaching. Suppose all or most of the shareholders of a company are also its directors. This would typically occur where a partnership business was incorporated, or a small number of joint venturers decided to start a new business, in the form of a limited company, in which all or some would take an active part. The former partners, or joint venturers, might simply adopt Table A articles. Under such articles, a simple majority would have the right to remove any director from office, and a winding-up would require a three-quarters' majority. Suppose a simple majority voted to remove one of the director/shareholders from his office as director. This would have unfortunate consequences for the shareholder concerned, since he would lose his right to remuneration. Such a step, however, might well be justified by good business reasons, for example lack of confidence in the shareholder's performance or general incompatibility between that shareholder and the others which has only manifested itself in the course of trading. Even if the majority shareholders made no offer to purchase the shares of the excluded shareholder at a fair value, it would nevertheless appear drastic to wind the company up on the basis that from the inception of the company the excluded shareholder had reasonably expected to remain in salaried office.

[17] At p. 380C–E.
[18] See the discussion of this subject in the context of unfair prejudice petitions: Chap. 4, para. 4–036 onwards. See also para. 3–026 below.

3–016 In *Re Westbourne Galleries*,[19] where the company was an incorporated partnership business and the ex-partners then fell out with each other, the Court of Appeal, consisting of Russell, Megaw and Buckley L.J.J., held that a minority shareholder removed as a director could not obtain a winding-up order on the just and equitable ground, even if all the shareholders had reasonable expectations to remain in salaried office, "unless it be shown that the power was not exercised bona fide in the interests of the company, or that the grounds for exercising the powers were such that no reasonable man could think that the removal was in the interests of the company." These words were clearly derived from the principles applicable to "fraud on minority," and in particular from the Court of Appeal judgment in *Greenhalgh* v. *Arderne*.[20] The decision of the Court of Appeal in *Re Westbourne Galleries* was, however, unanimously overruled by the House of Lords.[21]

In the House of Lords, it was argued by the minority shareholder that the court should apply partnership principles and therefore decree a dissolution in the case of the exclusion of a partner. The majority shareholders argued that the court should apply the articles of association, and should not introduce qualifications thereto by analogy with partnership cases. Their Lordships preferred the former arguments and made a winding-up order.

3–017 Lord Cross held:

> "The argument upon which counsel for the respondent chiefly relied in support of the decision of the Court of Appeal was quite different. Mr. Ebrahimi, he said, consented to the conversion of the partnership into a limited company. Even though he became, because George Nazar was taken in, only a minority shareholder he could have safeguarded his position by procuring the insertion in the articles of a provision 'weighting' the voting power of his shares on any question touching his retention of office as director: see *Bushell* v. *Faith* [1970] A.C. 1099. He must, therefore, be taken to have accepted the risk that if he and Mr. Nazar fell out he would be at Mr. Nazar's mercy. There might be force in this argument if there was any evidence to show that the minds of the parties were directed to the point; but there is no such evidence and the probability is that no one gave a moment's thought to the change in relative strength of their respective positions brought about by the conversion of the partnership into a company. It was not suggested that Mr. Ebrahimi had been guilty of any misconduct such as would justify one partner

[19] [1971] 1 Ch. 799 (C.A.); [1973] A.C. 360 (H.L.).
[20] See Chap. 2, para. 2–008 above.
[21] [1973] A.C. 360.

in expelling another under an expulsion clause contained in partnership articles. All that happened was that without one being more to blame than the other the two could no longer work together in harmony. Had no company been formed Mr. Ebrahimi could have had the partnership wound up and though Mr. Nazar and his son were entitled in law to oust him from his directorship and deprive him of his income they could only do so subject to Mr. Ebrahimi's right to obtain equitable relief in the form of a winding up order under section 222(f). I would, therefore, allow the appeal."[22]

The petitioner must, however, come to the court with "clean hands," the remedy being an equitable one. In the words of Lord Cross:

"if the breakdown in confidence between [the members] appears to have been due to [the petitioner's] misconduct he cannot insist on the company being wound up . . .."[23]

3–018 Lord Wilberforce, who gave the leading judgment, which has had great influence in this area of the law, may have regarded the facts as stronger in the petitioner's favour, and he referred in particular to the majority shareholder's refusal to recognise the petitioner as a partner.[24] He made it clear, however, that the court was entitled to imply equitable constraints upon the exercise of rights set out in the articles of association or the Companies Acts. He held:

"My Lords, in my opinion these authorities represent a sound and rational development of the law which should be endorsed. The foundation of it all lies in the words 'just and equitable' and, if there is any respect in which some of the cases may be open to criticism, it is that the courts may sometimes have been too timorous in giving them full force. The words are a recognition of the fact that a limited company is more than a mere legal entity, with a personality in law of its own: that there is room in company law for recognition of the fact that behind it, or amongst it, there are individuals, with rights, expectations and obligations *inter se* which are not necessarily submerged in the company structure. That structure is defined by the Companies Act and by the articles of association by which shareholders agree to be bound. In most companies and in most contexts, this definition is sufficient and exhaustive, equally so whether the company is large or small. The 'just and equitable' provision does not, as the respondents suggest, entitle one party to disregard the obligation he assumes by entering a company, nor the court to dispense him from it. It does, as equity always does, enable the court to subject the exercise of legal rights to equitable considerations;

[22] [1973] A.C. 360, at pp. 386F–387B.
[23] At p. 387G. See *Vujnovich* v. *Vujnovich* (1989) 5 B.C.C. 740.
[24] [1973] A.C. 360, at p. 381C–D.

> considerations, that is, of a personal character arising between one individual and another, which may make it unjust, or inequitable, to insist on legal rights, or to exercise them in a particular way."[25]

Lord Wilberforce went on to explain the circumstances which might justify a winding-up order:

> "It would be impossible, and wholly undesirable, to define the circumstances in which these considerations may arise. Certainly the fact that a company is a small one, or a private company, is not enough. There are very many of these where the association is a purely commercial one, of which it can safely be said that the basis of association is adequately and exhaustively laid down in the articles. The superimposition of equitable considerations requires something more, which typically may include one, or probably more, of the following elements: (i) an association formed or continued on the basis of a personal relationship, involving mutual confidence—this element will often be found where a pre-existing partnership has been converted into a limited company; (ii) an agreement, or understanding, that all, or some (for there may be 'sleeping' members), of the shareholders shall participate in the conduct of the business; (iii) restriction upon the transfer of the members' interest in the company—so that if confidence is lost, or one member is removed from management, he cannot take out his stake and go elsewhere."[26]

He concluded:

> "The just and equitable provision nevertheless comes to his assistance if he can point to, and prove, some special underlying obligation of his fellow member(s) in good faith, or confidence, that so long as the business continues he shall be entitled to management participation, an obligation so basic that, if broken, the conclusion must be that the association must be dissolved."[27]

3–019 It is not every small private company that will justify the implication of a "special underlying obligation that so long as the business continues he shall be entitled to management participation." In *Re A Company (No. 3096 of 1987)*[28] Peter Gibson J. held that no such obligation arose in the case of a private company formed by two husband-and-wife teams. In that case, the articles of association contained common pre-emption provisions and further provided that a shareholder should give a transfer

[25] At p. 379A–D.
[26] At p. 379E–G.
[27] At p. 380D–E.
[28] (1988) 4 B.C.C. 80.

notice thereunder if he ceased to be in the employment of the company. A similar conclusion had been reached on similar facts in *Re XYZ Ltd.*[29]

3–020 In *Re R. A. Noble (Clothing) Ltd.*[30] Nourse J. held that the circumstances of that case did give rise to "an implied agreement or an understanding that [the petitioner] should participate in all major decisions relating to the company's affairs." He went on to hold that the petitioner was entitled to a winding-up order, on the ground that, although he was partly at fault and the respondent shareholder was not guilty of "underhand" conduct, the respondent's conduct "was the substantial cause of the destruction of mutual confidence involved in the personal relationship"[31] between the two equal shareholders. It is noteworthy that, unlike *Re Westbourne Galleries*, this was not a case where the petitioner had been removed as a director. Rather, the complaint was that he had not been consulted on important matters. It is submitted that this case is support for the proposition that, in the case of a quasi-partnership, it is sufficient ground for a winding-up order that:

(1) the majority shareholder has run the company without consulting the other; and
(2) this has caused the breakdown of the relationship of trust and confidence.

3–021 In *Tay Bok Choon* v. *Tahanson*[32] a shareholder, who held one-quarter of the issued share capital of a private company, was removed from office as a director. The Privy Council held that there was an implied obligation on the part of the majority shareholders "to allow the petitioner to participate in management and to be a director unless by withdrawal of his support or for some other good reason a change in management and control became necessary."[33] In that case, the petitioner had provided considerable financial support to the company and his co-shareholders, and it was this consideration that carried weight with the court.

(2) *Loss of Confidence*

3–022 Where a minority shareholder can show a justifiable loss of confidence in the probity of the board of directors, then the court may make a winding-up order. It is submitted, however, that the facts will have to be fairly extreme to justify this course, unless there has been breach of some underlying obligation as in *Re Westbourne Galleries*.

[29] [1987] 1 W.L.R. 102.
[30] [1983] B.C.L.C. 273, 291f.
[31] At p. 291f–g.
[32] [1987] B.C.L.C. 472; [1987] 1 W.L.R. 413.
[33] At p. 475g–h.

3–023 In *Loch* v. *John Blackwood Ltd.*[34] the facts were, indeed, extreme. The board was dominated by the majority shareholder whose acts led inevitably to the conclusion that he regarded the company as the product of his own labours and was trying to buy out the minority shareholders, who were not directors, at an undervalue. The company was a small private company where the shareholders were related by family. The Privy Council held:

> "It is undoubtedly true that as the foundation of applications for winding up, on the 'just and equitable' rule, there must lie a justifiable lack of confidence in the conduct and management of the company's affairs. But this lack of confidence must be grounded on conduct of the directors, not in regard to their private life or affairs, but in regard to the company's business. Furthermore the lack of confidence must spring not from dissatisfaction at being outvoted on the business affairs or on what is called the domestic policy of the company. On the other hand, wherever the lack of confidence is rested on a lack of probity in the conduct of the company's affairs, then the former is justified by the latter, and it is under the statute just and equitable, that the company be wound up."[35]

The Privy Council had no difficulty in finding justifiable lack of confidence in the probity of the majority shareholder and made a winding-up order.

(3) *Deadlock*

3–024 Total deadlock in the management of the affairs of the company is unusual. If there is an equality of votes at a meeting of the directors or members, the chairman of the meeting will often have a casting vote. If there is deadlock at board level for any reason, then the powers of the board will become exercisable by the members in general meeting.[36] Where there is total deadlock, in the absence of some other remedy[37] the court would have little option but to order a winding-up.

3–025 The court will also order a winding-up where there is practical, although not total, deadlock in the management of the affairs of the company. In *Re Yenidge Tobacco Co. Ltd.*[38] there were two equal shareholders and directors. The articles of association provided for a reference to arbitration of any dispute between the shareholders. The

[34] [1924] A.C. 783. See by way of analogy s. 35 of The Partnership Act, and *Lindley on Partnership* (15th ed.), pp. 704–707.
[35] At p. 788.
[36] *Barron* v. *Potter* [1914] 1 Ch. 895.
[37] Such as an order on the unfair prejudice ground.
[38] [1916] 2 Ch. 426.

relationship of trust and confidence between them broke down, to such an extent that one would not speak to the other. Lord Cozens-Hardy M.R. referred to partnership principles, whereby:

> "(A)ll that is necessary to satisfy the Court that it is impossible for the partners to place that confidence in each other which each has a right to expect, and that such impossibility has not been caused by the person seeking to take advantage of it."[39]

Warrington L.J. held:

> "(I)n a case like the present, where there are only two persons interested, where there are no shareholders other than those two, where there are no means of overruling by the action of a general meeting of shareholders the trouble which is occasioned by the quarrels of the two directors and shareholders, the company ought to be wound up if there exists such a ground as would be sufficient for the dissolution of a private partnership at the suit of one of the partners against the other. Such ground exists in the present case."[40]

(4) Miscellaneous

3–026 A much more common case than deadlock is that of a quasi-partnership, in the sense of that expression as used in *Re Westbourne Galleries*, where there is no state of deadlock, whether practical or total, but the relationship of trust and confidence between directors has broken down. In those circumstances, it is doubtful whether that fact in itself is sufficient to justify a winding-up order. The outcome may depend on whether the disgruntled minority shareholder has a right of management participation or not. If he does not, then it is submitted that he must establish grounds for winding-up on the authority of *Lock* v. *John Blackwood*. If he does have such a right, and he is removed as a director or there is some other substantial interference with that right, then it appears that a winding-up order will be made: *Re Westbourne Galleries* and *Re Noble & Son (Clothing) Ltd.*[41] What if the minority shareholder has such a right but, despite the breakdown in trust and confidence, there is no attempt to interfere with that right? It could be argued, on the following grounds, that the minority shareholder should still be entitled to wind-up the company:

(1) the majority shareholder, if he had removed the minority shareholder as a director, may have acted in a way that any prudent businessperson would have done; and
(2) the right of management participation is deprived of much meaning if the relationship of trust and confidence has broken down.

[39] At p. 430.
[40] At p. 435.
[41] See para. 3–020 above.

As will be seen in the case of unfair prejudice petitions,[42] the court will have regard to the severance terms offered to the minority shareholder at the time of the breakdown. Thus, if there has been an irretrievable breakdown of relations between executive quasi-partners, where the minority shareholder offers to resign if his shares in the company are purchased at a fair value, then it is arguable that a court would make a winding-up order on the just and equitable ground, if the majority shareholder without good reason declined the offer.

3–027 This submission is supported by the judgments of Hoffmann J. in a number of cases which are discussed in the context of unfair prejudice petitions.[43] As is noted there, however, there may be a catch for the minority shareholder if the majority offer to buy him out at an independent valuation: the minority cannot insist that the valuation be without a discount for a minority shareholding.

3–028 In *Re A Company (No. 00370 of 1987) ex p. Glossop*[44] it was alleged by a minority shareholder in a family company, who had no right to management participation, that the directors of the company had failed to pay reasonable dividends out of the very large profits of the company. Harman J. held that this allegation was capable of founding a petition to wind up the company on the just and equitable ground. The learned judge first noted that there was no longer any tax disincentive to distributing profits by way of dividends. He held:

> "On that basis, (leaving aside the question of taxation, which cannot, in my view, change the basic purpose, although it may make the purpose difficult if not impossible to effect) it is, in my judgment, right to say that directors have a duty to consider how much they can properly distribute to members. They have a duty, as I see it, to remember that the members are the owners of the company, that the profits belong to the members, and that, subject to the proper needs of the company to ensure that it is not trading in a risky manner and that there are adequate reserves for commercial purposes, by and large the trading profits ought to be distributed by way of dividends. No doubt in practical terms shareholders will have a difficult case to make if directors, not considering their own personal pocket, not benefiting themselves in some capacity (*e.g.* by paying out to themselves remuneration in excess of that which should legitimately

[42] Chap. 4, para. 4–055 onwards.
[43] See at Chap. 4, para. 4–060.
[44] [1988] 1 W.L.R. 1068. See paras. 4–032 and 4–043 below.

be paid so that their remuneration is limited to that which would be paid to ordinary people in the market performing those functions), simply pile up profits in the company and do not distribute them by way of dividend. Nonetheless members can, in my view, if those facts were adequately proved, make the company the subject of a petition for a just and equitable winding up; because the proper and legitimate expectations of members have not been applied, but have been defeated."[45]

3–029 Thus, the right to management participation is not the only "proper and legitimate expectation" that a minority shareholder may be found to have in the particular circumstances of a case. Another such expectation is the right to participate in profits by way of dividend. Other circumstances may give rise to other expectations.

Pre-emption Articles and Reasonable Offers

3–030 The consequences of the presence of rights of pre-emption in the company's articles of association, and those of offers to buy the petitioner's shares whether or not pursuant to such rights of pre-emption, are discussed in the context of unfair prejudice petitions.[46] If the existence of these circumstances is sufficient to justify the dismissal of an unfair prejudice petition, it will almost invariably follow that a winding-up petition will be dismissed. In many cases, a petition will seek an order on the unfair prejudice ground under section 461 of the 1985 Act, alternatively a winding-up order.

Relationship with Other Remedies

3–031 The provisions of section 125(2) of the 1986 Act have already been noted.[47] The unfair prejudice remedy under Part XVII of the 1985 Act has greatly increased the options available to a minority shareholder. In many cases, such as breakdown in confidence and exclusion from management, the minority will have grounds both for a winding-up order on the just and equitable ground and relief on the unfair prejudice ground. The petition will in such cases usually seek the two forms of relief as alternatives. When the dispute is heard, the court will invariable make an order for the purchase of the petitioner's shares (if that is the relief claimed and the petition is successful) rather than making a winding-up

[45] At p. 1076C–F.
[46] See Chap. 4, para. 4–047 below onwards.
[47] See para. 3–001 above.

order, because the former remedy is generally less drastic and fully compensates the petitioner.[48]

3–032 The company, however, will be anxious not to have the winding-up petition hanging over its head pending trial. Only, however, where it is plain and obvious that the unfair prejudice remedy is the appropriate remedy rather than winding-up will the court strike out a winding-up petition *in limine*. There are significant differences between the two remedies.[49] For example the conduct complained of in unfair prejudice petitions must be the "conduct of the company's affairs," whereas there is no such requirement in just and equitable petitions.[50]

3–033 In *Re A Company (No. 001363 of 1988)*[51] the company was a quasi-partnership and the minority shareholder had been removed from office as a director on a breakdown in relations. He presented a winding-up petition on the just and equitable ground, and the company applied to strike it out on the ground, *inter alia*, that relief on the unfair prejudice ground was more appropriate. Warner J., in rejecting this application, held that it was irrelevant that the forms of relief were wider on an unfair prejudice petition and that it was more likely that the court would grant relief under section 459 of the 1985 Act. The learned judge accepted that the winding-up petition might inconvenience the company and continued:

> "But does it follow that one should hold that either generally or in a particular kind of case a person in S-J's [the petitioner] position, someone who claims that his equitable rights, as it were, as a quasi-partner have been infringed, should refrain from presenting a winding-up petition? Mr. Dutton [counsel for the petitioner] points out, rightly, that the decision of the House of Lords in the *Westbourne Galleries* case still stands. It has not been negatived by legislation. It still means that that remedy is available to a person who is aggrieved in the way in which S-J is aggrieved. True, at the hearing of the petition the judge may, on the full facts when they are found, hold that it would be unreasonable to grant him the remedy of a winding-up and that he should pursue his remedy under section 459, but it is a very strong thing to say, on an application to strike out, that it is plain and obvious that a petitioner is behaving unreasonably in seeking a winding-up order."[52]

3–034 There will be exceptional cases, however, where it is plain and obvious, from the beginning, that the petitioner has an adequate alternative

[48] See *Re Cumana* [1986] B.C.L.C. 430, where the respondents would have preferred a winding-up, rather than be bankrupted by a share purchase order.
[49] See *Re Noble & Sons (Clothing) Ltd.*, [1983] B.C.L.C. 273.
[50] See *Coulson Sanderson & Ward Ltd.* v. *Ward* [1986] 2 B.C.C. 99,207,99,217.
[51] (1989) 5 B.C.C. 18.
[52] At p. 25D–F.

remedy and that he is unreasonably pursuing a winding-up petition. In *Re A Company (No. 003028 of 1987)*[53] the company was a quasi-partnership where two quasi-partners had entered into a joint venture agreement. The majority purported to remove the minority from office as director on the ground of serious misconduct. The minority commenced a writ action claiming, *inter alia*, damages for breach of contract and also presented a winding-up petition. The latter was struck out by Scott J. The learned judge held that the writ action would be determinative of the parties' rights. If it succeeded, the minority would be entitled to a winding-up order as a matter of right as a creditor. If it failed, it would be because the minority shareholder:

> "will, by his own manifestly unreasonable conduct in interrupting the proper conduct of the business of the company, have brought on himself his own dismissal . . . He could not rely on his own misconduct in order to invite the court on the just and equitable ground to order the company to be wound up. In that event, the winding-up petition would be bound to fail with the Queen's Bench action."[54]

Procedure

3–035 The procedure for the presentation and prosecution of a winding-up petition by a shareholder on the unfair prejudice ground is governed by Rules 4.22 to 4.24 of the Insolvency Rules 1986. The jurisdiction of county courts is limited by section 117 of the 1986 Act. Only certain county courts[55] even have that limited jurisdiction and the usual practice in anything but the most straightforward case is to present the petition in the High Court.[56] The High Court has unlimited jurisdiction and the matter is assigned to the Chancery Division, Companies Court. It is important to note that no affidavits should be filed in support of the petition until the first return date for directions, and that advertisement should only take place pursuant to the specific direction of the court, which will invariably not be made.

3–036 Upon presentation of a winding-up petition, section 127 of the 1986 Act comes into operation in theory. The effect of this section is that, in the event of a winding-up, all dispositions of the company after the presentation of the petition are avoided unless the court otherwise directs. In theory, given the risk that the court might make an order on

[53] [1988] B.C.L.C. 282.
[54] At p. 295g–i.
[55] See Civil Courts Order 1983 (S.I. 1983/713) and subsequent orders.
[56] Some District Registries have winding-up jurisdiction.

the petition, the company should apply for a court order validating all dispositions in the ordinary course of business pending the determination of the petition. Such an order will usually be granted if asked for. It would be unwise for the petitioner to oppose such an order, since such opposition will probably be seen as an attempt to use the petition as an instrument of oppression. In many cases, however, the company will not bother to obtain a validating order, especially if it is known that the petitioner will be bought off if the petition succeeds. The directors of the company run the risk, however, of being liable personally for any disposition of the company's property, if a winding-up order is made and the court declines to validate the disposition retrospectively. The company may be forced by its bankers to apply for a validation order if the bankers learn of the petition, for the bankers will be similarly at risk in the event of a winding-up order.[57]

[57] See *Re Gray's Inn Construction* [1980] 1 W.L.R. 711. See also *Re Crossmore Electrical & Civil Engineering Ltd.* (1989) 5 B.C.C. 37.

Chapter 4

THE UNFAIR PREJUDICE REMEDY

4–001 Section 459(1) of the 1985 Act (which forms part of a group of provisions contained in part XVII of the 1985 Act) provides a remedy to a shareholder of a company in circumstances where:

> " . . . the company's affairs are being or have been conducted in a manner which is unfairly prejudicial to the interests of some part of the members (including at least himself) or that any actual or proposed act or omission of the company (including an act or omission on its behalf) is or would be so prejudicial."

If the above circumstances are established, the court "may make such order as it thinks fit for giving relief in respect of the matters complained of."

The discretion and powers bestowed upon the court by the provisions of Part XVII of the 1985 Act are exceptionally wide. As was noted in the Cohen Report published in 1944,[1] there are many examples of abuse of position by majority shareholders and it is impossible to make provision for each example. Once it was accepted as a matter of principle that there should be a remedy, other than by way of winding-up or a derivative action, against such abuses, then it was inevitable that the court would have to have a wide discretion.

Section 210 of the 1948 Act, the predecessor of Part XVII of the 1985 Act, was, however, limited by its connection with the winding-up remedy. This remedy (now repealed) against oppression of minorities was probably intended[2] and was certainly interpreted[3] to be available only in circumstances where the court could have made a winding-up order. No such limitation applies under the current law contained in Part XVII of the 1985 Act, and this is the fundamental difference between the old and new law.

[1] Cmd. 6659.
[2] Para. 60 and Recommendations at p. 95 of the Cohen Report.
[3] *Re Bellador Silk Ltd.* [1965] 1 W.L.R. 1051.

Locus Standi

4–002 In order to present a petition for relief under Part XVII of the 1985 Act ("an unfair prejudice petition"), a person must have the *locus standi* prescribed by section 459 of the Act. Section 459(1) provides that a "member" of the company may petition. Section 459(2) then provides:

> "The provisions of this Part apply to a person who is not a member of a company but to whom shares in the company have been transferred or transmitted by operation of law, as those provisions apply to a member of the company . . .."

The above provisions can lead to arbitrary results. A "member" of a company is defined by section 22 of the 1985 Act to be a subscriber to the memorandum of association, and "(e)very other person who agrees to become a member of the company and whose name is entered in its register of members."

4–003 The principal qualification for the right to present a petition is, therefore, the fact that the petitioner is either a subscriber to the memorandum (who will often merely be a company formation agent) or entered as a member in the company's register of members. This has the advantage of certainty; it will invariably be clear from the company's register of members (assuming it has not been lost or destroyed) who are the persons registered as members at a given time. On the other hand, since errors may well occur in the making of entries in the register of members and these errors may well be the responsibility of the majority shareholders who are the intended respondents to the petition, the conclusiveness of the register of members for this purpose has the result that a person who alleges that the register of members incorrectly omits him as a member must, before presenting a petition, bring an action for rectification of the register of members pursuant to section 359 of the 1985 Act. The question then arises whether that person, having obtained rectification, can complain about conduct unfairly prejudicial to himself at a time when he was not registered as a member but was entitled to rectification of the register. It is implicit in *Re Quickdome*[4] that such a person can complain about that conduct, although obviously much will depend on the circumstances. The facts of that case will be dealt with below, but it is sufficient in this context to observe that Mervyn Davies J. did not feel any reluctance in striking out the petition in that case, since he bore in mind the words of Brightman J. in a case concerned with *locus standi* to present a winding-up petition:

[4] [1988] B.C.L.C. 370.

"By dismissing the petition the court is not driving a litigant from the judgment seat, or doing any injustice to him. The court will be merely requiring him to establish his right to present a petition before he is permitted to take a step which has such an immediate and potentially damaging effect on the company."[5]

4–004 Section 459(2) significantly widens the *locus standi* requirements of an unfair prejudice petition. For example, it is clear that a person to whom shares have been validly transferred by a proper instrument of transfer but whom the directors have refused to register as a member has *locus standi* to present a petition, although it may be more difficult for him to assert that he has suffered unfair prejudice. The courts have, however, applied a strict interpretation to the provision in section 459(2) that shares must have been "transferred or transmitted by operation of law" to the intended petitioner.

4–005 In *Re A Company (No. 007828 of 1985)* Harman J. held:

"In my view, transmission by operation of law means some act in the law by which the legal estate passes even though there be some further act (such as registration) to be done; and in my view the mere allegation that there arises a constructive trust—remembering that a constructive trust is frequently a matter of a remedy supplied by a court by way of imposition upon the conscience of the person affected, rather than an existing act in the law—cannot possibly amount to a transmission by operation of law."[6]

In that case, it had been argued on behalf of the petitioner that they had agreed to acquire shares in the company, were the equitable owners of the shares, and consequently were persons to whom the shares had been transmitted by operation of law. This argument was rejected.

4–006 The typical case of a person to whom shares had been transmitted by operation of law would be a person entitled to shares upon the death or bankruptcy of a shareholder.

4–007 In *Re A Company (No. 007828 of 1985) (supra)* it was apparently common ground between the parties that a "transfer" of shares involved usually an instrument of transfer. This construction was applied by Hoffmann J. in *Re A Company (No. 003160 of 1986)*.[7] After noting that the language of section 459(2) echoed the language of section 183 of the 1985 Act, he held:

[5] *Re J.N.2 Ltd.* [1978] 1 W.L.R. 183, 188.
[6] (1986) 2 B.C.C. 98,951, 98,954.
[7] (1986) 2 B.C.C. 99,276; [1986] B.C.L.C. 391. See also *Theakston* v. *London Trust plc* [1984] B.C.L.C. 390; *Re Scott's Trustees* [1959] A.C. 763, 778.

"In my judgment the word 'transferred' in section 459(2) requires at least that a proper instrument of transfer should have been executed and delivered to the transferee or the company in respect of the shares in question. It is not sufficient that there should be an agreement for transfer."[8]

4–008 In *Re Quickdome* (*supra*), the company had been acquired off-the-shelf, and, as is common procedure, the two company formation agents, who were the nominal subscribers, executed and delivered stock transfer forms in blank. The petitioner alleged that the company was a joint venture between the respondent and the petitioner's husband and that the two subscriber shares were to be registered in the names of the petitioner and the respondent's wife, as nominees for their respective husbands. The respondent alleged, in contrast, that the two subscriber shares were to be registered in the names of the respondent's wife and the petitioner's husband, as nominees for the respondent and the respondent's wife respectively. Mervyn Davies J. held that the petitioner had no *locus standi* to present a petition under Part XVII of the 1985 Act, since she was not registered as a shareholder and was not named as a transferee in the stock transfer forms. In applying *Re A Company (No. 003160 of 1986) (supra)* he held:

" . . . I cannot say that a proper instrument of transfer has been executed. The transfer relied on is in blank as to the name of the transferee."[9]

As has been noted above, the effect of this decision is essentially a procedural one only. The petitioner was required first to establish by an action her claim to be the transferee of a share in the company. Having succeeded in such an action, she could then bring her petition.

4–009 Issues that both *Re A Company (No. 003160 of 1986)* and *Re Quickdome (supra)* raise but do not decide concern the common situation of a joint venture between, say, A and Mr. and Mrs. B. In such a situation, for example, A and Mr. B. might be the active participants and directors, whilst Mr. B's shares are held by his wife as nominee. In such a case, can Mrs. B., as the member, complain about the unfair exclusion by A of Mr. B? On the one hand, it would appear strange that Mrs. B. should be entitled to the statutory remedy, when she has no beneficial interest in the capital of the company. On the other hand, it would appear strange that Mr. and Mrs. B. should be deprived of a remedy, simply because of the convenience of putting shares into Mrs. B's name, especially since the problem of *locus standi* could apparently be overcome by Mrs. B

[8] At p. 99,279.
[9] At p. 375a.

executing an instrument of transfer in favour of Mr. B (assuming, of course, that such a strategem did not have the unwelcome result of invoking pre-emption provisions in the articles of association of the company). In *Re A Company (No. 003160 of 1986) (supra)* Hoffmann J., having held that the husband had no *locus standi,* observed *obiter* that he doubted whether this made any difference in practice.

> "The jurisdiction to remedy conduct 'unfairly prejudicial' to the interests of members enables the court to protect not only the rights of members under the constitution of the company but also the 'rights, expectations and obligations' of the individual shareholders *inter se*. (Compare Lord Wilberforce in *Ebrahimi* v. *Westbourne Galleries Ltd.* [1972] 2 All E.R. 492 at 500, [1973] A.C. 360 at 379). In the typical case of the corporate quasi-partnership, these will include the expectations that the member will be able to participate in the management of the company and share in its profits through salaried employment. As at present advised, I do not see why, if such was the understanding between the parties, it should not also include an expectation that a nominee member's husband and beneficiary should enjoy such rights and benefits."[10]

It is, therefore, submitted that, in the case mentioned in the preceding paragraph, Mrs. B. can complain about the unfair exclusion of Mr. B.

4–010 Another issue, which is strictly not one of *locus standi* but is connected thereto, concerns the case of a member who is registered as such but who is alleged by the intended respondent to be erroneously registered as such or to be a nominee for the respondent or a third party. Will the petition be stayed or struck out pending resolution of this dispute? It is submitted that in some cases it may be convenient to stay the petition and in other cases to determine the dispute on the hearing of the petition. The general rule, in the case of a contributory's winding-up petition, is to require determination of the dispute before presentation of the petition[11]. It may be that this general rule will have less force in the case of an unfair prejudice petition although it should be noted that the court has power to make a winding-up order even under this Part. On the special facts of *Re Garage Door Associates*[12] Mervyn Davies J. refused to strike out a petition where the petitioner was alleged to have no beneficial interest in the capital of the company. In that case, one of the special facts was that the respondent to the petition in question had himself presented a cross-

[10] (1986) 2 B.C.C. 99,276, at p. 99,281.
[11] Para. 3–007 above.
[12] [1983] B.C.L.C. 164.

petition, which raised the dispute of beneficial ownership in shares. In the absence of such special facts, it is submitted that it is likely that the court would be inclined to stay a petition until the dispute of beneficial ownership had been determined.[13]

Final Orders

4–011 The court's powers are extremely wide in the event that it is found that the affairs of the company have been conducted in an unfairly prejudicial manner. Section 461(1) provides:

> "If the court is satisfied that a petition under this Part is well founded, it may make such order as it thinks fit for giving relief in respect of the matters complained of."

Orders will normally be made against the company and its present members, but the court has power to make an order in appropriate circumstances against a former member.[14]

4–012 Section 461(2) specifies certain remedies available:

> "(2) Without prejudice to the generality of subsection (1), the court's order may—
>
> (a) regulate the conduct of the company's affairs in the future,
>
> (b) require the company to refrain from doing or continuing an act complained of by the petitioner or to do an act which the petitioner has complained it has omitted to do,
>
> (c) authorise civil proceedings to be brought in the name and on behalf of the company by such person or persons and on such terms as the court may direct,
>
> (d) provide for the purchase of the shares of any members of the company by other members or by the company itself and, in the case of a purchase by the company itself, the reduction of the company's capital accordingly."

Sub-sections (3) and (4) of section 461 make provision for orders requiring the company to alter its memorandum or articles of association.

4–013 The most important remedy is an order for the purchase of the petitioner's shares either by another member or the company. Such an order has the advantage that the petitioner can realise the value of his interest in the company without having the company wound up, and the effect of the order upon the purchasers, who *ex hypothesi* receive full

[13] But see *Re A Company (No. 001363 of 1988)* (1989) 5 B.C.C. 18.
[14] *Re A Company* [1986] B.C.L.C. 68, 71e–f.

value for the price paid for the shares, is kept to a minimum.[15] If the petitioner is entitled to a winding-up order on the just and equitable ground (see Chapter 3 above) it is likely to be irrelevant whether he is also liable to succeed on the unfair prejudice ground, since the respondents will usually choose to buy him out rather than suffer a winding-up.

The question of the proper valuation of the shares to be purchased, which is clearly central to any case in which a purchase order is sought, is dealt with below.[16]

4–014 In certain circumstances, the petitioner will seek an order that some or all of the other members sell their shares to him, as opposed to their buying his shares. There is no reason why the court should not make such an order, but it is submitted that in most circumstances the court would be more inclined to order the purchase of the petitioner's shares, since it is one thing to allow the petitioner to realise his interest in the company and quite another thing compulsorily to expropriate the interests of other members, who will usually constitute the majority. An order for the compulsory expropriation of a majority shareholder's interest by a minority shareholder was made, on terms, in *Re A Company (No. 00789 of 1987)*.[17]

In *Re Ringtower Holdings plc*[18] Peter Gibson J. held that it was inconceivable to make an order for the purchase of the shares of the majority where:

(1) the petitioners together only held about 5 per cent. of the shares;
(2) the petitioner did not come to the court with clean hands, and there would be the potential for further conflict in the future; and
(3) it was plain and obvious that the petitioners ought to go in view of the breakdown of relations, the smallness of their holdings, the opposition of the respondents including senior managers and the absence of the petitioners from the company for 18 months.[19]

4–015 Orders that shares be bought or sold may be the only means of remedying unfair prejudice in the cases of small private companies. As has already been noted, however, there is no substantial limit to the court's powers. In *Re McGuinness*[20] the Court of Session ordered the directors of a public company to convene an extraordinary general

[15] For an example of a case where the effect of the order was very drastic indeed for the purchaser, who would very much have preferred a winding-up, see *Re Cumana* [1986] B.C.L.C. 430.
[16] Para. 4–066.
[17] (1989) 5 B.C.C. 652
[18] (1989) 5 B.C.C. 82,103.
[19] See also *Re A Company (No. 006834 of 1988)* (1989) 5 B.C.C. 218.
[20] (1988) B.C.C. 161.

meeting of the company on a specified date and to appoint a firm of accountants as independent scrutineers.

4–016 A good example of a case where the appropriate remedy would be other than by way of a share purchase order is *Re Harmer*.[21] In that case, the court made detailed orders for the future regulation of the company's affairs.

Interlocutory Orders

(1) *The General Powers of Court*

4–017 As in all other actions, the court has the power to make interlocutory orders by way of injunction or the appointment of a receiver "in all cases in which it appears to the court to be just and convenient to do so."[22] This is an area, *par excellence,* for the exercise of discretion by the court and much will depend on the particular facts of the case. For a discussion of the general principles which guide the court's discretion, reference should be made to the Supreme Court Practice.[23] The leading authority is *American Cyanamid* v. *Ethicon*.[24] In summary, the applicant must first show an arguable case. Having shown an arguable case, the applicant must then show that the balance of convenience favours the granting of an injunction. In considering the balance of convenience, the court must consider the adequacy of damages, to the applicant and respondent respectively, in the event that the injunction is granted or refused, as the case may be.

4–018 As Hoffmann J. pointed out, however, in *Re Posgate & Denby (Agencies) Ltd.*,[25] those principles cannot be applied literally to an unfair prejudice petition, since the common law remedy of damages is not available to a petitioner. In that case, the learned judge found that the petitioner had failed to show an arguable case.[26] Even on the assumption that an arguable case had been shown, he held that it was not "just and convenient"[27] to grant the injunction sought. The facts were that the petitioner complained about the proposed sales of the company's assets to companies in which the directors and majority shareholders were interested. The learned judge held that the petitioner would be adequately compensated, if it ultimately was established that the sales were at an

[21] [1959] 1 W.L.R. 62. Compare *Re A Company (No. 00789 of 1987)* (1989) 5 B.C.C. 792.
[22] s. 37 of the Supreme Court Act 1981 and s. 38 of the County Court Act 1984.
[23] See R.S.C., Ord. 29.
[24] [1975] A.C. 496.
[25] [1987] B.C.L.C. 8, 15d.
[26] See para. 4–029 below.
[27] At p. 15d.

undervalue, by an order for the purchase of his shares "at a price which reflects the value they would have had if the unfairly prejudicial conduct had not taken place,"[28] whereas there was a risk of irreparable harm to the respondents if the injunction was granted.

4–019 In *Re A Company*[29] Harman J. observed, *obiter*, that as a general rule it is desirable to preserve the status quo in the case of a petition under Part XVII of the 1985 Act:

> "I would add that, as it seems to me, in cases of litigation under s.75 [of the 1980 Act] it is most desirable that the position of the company be not altered or disturbed more than is absolutely essential, between the presentation and the hearing of the petition. The existing share structure, the existing contractual rights, the present service contracts and so forth, should in my judgment be maintained as they are pending the determination of the litigation. There might be circumstances where change was essential, but if possible the existing position should be preserved. In my judgment, that is a factor which in these matters arising under contributories patterns is particularly powerful and has more than the normal 'Cyanamid' (*American Cyanamid Co.* v. *Ethicon Ltd.* [1975] 1 All E.R 504, [1975] A.C. 396) force in favour of preserving the status quo, since it is the very nature of this matter that the status quo must affect the remedy which may be available."[30]

As is apparent from the last sentence of this passage, the learned judge had in mind cases where the remedies available on the determination of the petition might be restricted by a change in the status quo.

(2) *Section 461 of the 1985 Act*

4–020 In *Re A Company (No. 004175 of 1986)*[31] the petitioner argued that the court had the power to make, in effect, an interim order for the purchase of his shares. Scott J. held that the court had no jurisdiction to make such an order. Scott J. held, *inter alia*:

> "A power for the court to anticipate a purchase order made pursuant to Section 461(2)(d) and, before the statutory criterion has been shown to be satisfied, to make an interim order for payment on account of the purchase price, would require in my judgment to be spelled out by clear words of statutory authority. There is none. . . . Under s.459(1) and s.461(1) and (2), the court may have jurisdiction

[28] At p. 15e.
[29] [1985] B.C.L.C. 80. For final hearing, see *Re Cumana* [1986] B.C.L.C. 430.
[30] At pp. 82i–83c.
[31] [1987] B.C.L.C. 574.

> to order payment to be made by the respondents to the petitioner. But that jurisdiction will not, in my judgment, arise until the specified statutory criterion has been satisfied. Until then the court does not, in my judgment, have jurisdiction to make any order for payment, whether interim or final . . . ."[32]

Upon the basis of this authority, it would appear that the court has no jurisdiction to make an interim order, for example, so as to "regulate the conduct of the company's affairs in the future" pursuant to section 461(2)(a) of the 1985 Act. On the other hand, however, the court would be able to achieve the same result under its general jurisdiction to grant interlocutory injunctions. Thus, there would appear to be no obstacle in principle to the grant, for example, of mandatory injunctions requiring the respondent to reappoint as a director, pending the hearing of the petition, a petitioner who has been removed from office.

(3) *Indemnity as to costs*[33]

4–021 In *Re Sherborne Park Residents Co. Ltd.*[34] a member presented an unfair prejudice petition to restrain a proposed issue of new shares which would alter the balance of votes in the company. The petitioner applied for an interlocutory order that the company indemnify the petitioner in respect of the costs of the petition. Hoffmann J. held that the petitioner's complaint was, in substance, not that a wrong had been done to the company but that a wrong had been done to him as an individual shareholder: the alleged breach of fiduciary duties by the directors might in theory be a breach of duty owed to the company but in substance was an infringement of a member's contractual rights under the company's articles.[35] The learned judge held that the jurisdiction to make orders for the indemnification of shareholders as to costs was limited to those cases where the company was the true plaintiff and the shareholder was suing on behalf of the company. Two points should be noted about this case. First, the learned judge clearly contemplated that, in an appropriate case, a petitioner under Part XVII of the 1985 Act might be entitled to such an order for indemnification, where the petition was in substance to protect the interests of the company: for example, where the petition sought to restrain a transaction disadvantageous to the company.[36] Secondly, a petitioner protecting his own interests might, if successful on his petition,

[32] At pp. 578h–579d.
[33] See "Derivative Actions" at para. 2–037 onwards.
[34] [1987] B.C.L.C. 82.
[35] At p. 84g.
[36] At p. 85a–c.

recover costs against the company on a common fund basis: see *Marks* v. *Estates & General Investments.*[37]

Unfair Prejudice

4–022 At the heart of the jurisdiction under Part XVII of the 1985 Act is the establishment of the relevant unfair prejudice, namely that the interests of some part of the members (including the petitioner) have been thereby unfairly prejudiced.

Before analysing this element, the following points should be noted:

(1) It is not necessary to show a course of conduct, nor one continuing at the date of the petition: an isolated past act or omission is sufficient.
(2) The court also has jurisdiction to remedy a proposed future act or omission.
(3) The actions complained of must consist of the conduct of "the company's affairs" or an "act or omission of the company (including an act or omission on its behalf) . . .."

In the great majority of cases it is clear that the conduct complained of is that of, or on behalf of, the company. Thus, if the directors of a company distribute the profits of the company to themselves in the guise of remuneration to the detriment of shareholders who are not directors, the conduct of the directors is clearly the conduct of the company. A definition of what constitutes conduct of the affairs of the company is bound to be largely tautologous. In *Re A Company (No. 001761 of 1986)*[38] Harman J. held:

> "Thus one must always analyse very carefully . . . what is the conduct in the company itself or by the company itself (whether it be a single act or whether it be a course of conduct matters not) to see that there was conduct in the company's own affairs . . . (T)he conduct complained of must be in the affairs of the very company in respect of which the petition is presented."[39]

That case provides examples of conduct which illustrate the distinction between conduct "in the company" and conduct "dehors the company."[40]

4–023 Conduct "in the company" is illustrated by the facts of the well-known case of *Scottish Co-operative Wholesale Society* v. *Meyer.*[41] In that case, in essence, the majority shareholder had set up a rival company and the

[37] [1976] 1 W.L.R. 380.
[38] [1987] B.C.L.C. 141.
[39] At p. 144f–g.
[40] At p. 148a.
[41] [1959] A.C. 324. And see *Re Stewarts (Brixton) Ltd.* [1985] B.C.L.C. 4.

board of directors, which it controlled, stood by and allowed the business of the company to decline. It was held that the inaction of the board with knowledge of the setting up of the rival company constituted conduct in the affairs of the company. That was a decision under section 210 of the 1948 Act, where the relevant test was whether there had been oppression in the conduct of the affairs of the company. Under section 459 of the 1985 Act, it is sufficient to show an omission of the company, so that it is clear that an omission on the part of the board of directors would be sufficient.

4–024 Conduct "dehors the company" is illustrated by the example of a director who steals cash from the company's safe.[42] This act would constitute conduct by a director in his personal capacity. Moreover, it would make no difference if he had abused his position as a director to effect the theft. It would, however, be otherwise if the director in question used his dominant position in the company to stifle any proceedings by the company against himself. In those circumstances, it would be that use of a dominant position that constituted the conduct complained of.

It is submitted that, as will appear from the following section, the limitation of Part XVII of the 1985 Act to corporate acts or omissions will rarely be significant, since the statutory test of conduct "unfairly prejudicial to the interests of some part of the members" would never be satisfied if the conduct complained of was not made up of corporate acts and omissions.

4–025 In order to satisfy the statutory test of unfair prejudice it must be shown that (1) the interests of (2) some part of the members, including the petitioner, have been (3) prejudiced (4) unfairly.

(1) *Interests*

4–026 It was repeatedly held, under section 210 of the 1948 Act, that the oppression to members had to be suffered by the petitioner in his capacity as a member as such and not, for example, as a director or creditor.[43] Furthermore, the courts drew a sharp distinction between oppression suffered as a member as opposed to as a director. Thus, a joint venturer in a small private company could not complain, for example, about his removal from the board by the majority shareholders, since his position as a member was regarded as unaffected. This distinction had become

[42] [1987] B.C.L.C. 141, at p. 148b.

[43] See *Buckley on the Companies Acts* (14th ed.), p. 491, and cases cited in n. 5. It is arguable, however, that these cases were inconsistent with *Scottish Co-op Wholesale Society* v. *Meyer* [1959] A.C. 324.

established before the House of Lords decision in *Re Westbourne Galleries*, where Lord Wilberforce took a wider view of the interests of members in small private companies. The hope was expressed that the courts would adopt a similarly wide view in relation to the "unfair prejudice" remedy.[44]

4–027 This hope has been fulfilled. In *Re A Company (No. 00477 of 1986)* Hoffmann J. held as follows, and it is worth citing this passage at length:

> "Counsel for the company submitted that the section must be limited to conduct which is unfairly prejudicial to the interests of the members as members. It cannot extend to conduct which is prejudicial to other interests of persons who happen to be members.
> In principle I accept this proposition, as did Lord Granchester Q.C. in *Re a Company* [1983] 2 All E.R 36, [1983] Ch. 178. But its application must take into account that the interests of a member are not necessarily limited to his strict legal rights under the constitution of the company. The use of the word 'unfairly' in s.459, like the use of the words 'just and equitable' in s.517(1)(g), enables the court to have regard to wider equitable considerations.
> As Lord Wilberforce said of the latter words in *Ebrahimi* v. *Westbourne Galleries* ([1972] 2 All E.R. 492 at 500, [1973] A.C. 360 at 379), they are a recognition of the fact that: ' . . . a limited company is more than a mere entity, with a personality in law of its own: that there is room in company law for recognition of the fact that behind it, or amongst it, there are individuals with rights, expectations and obligations *inter se* which are not necessarily submerged in the company structure.'
> Thus in the case of the managing director of a large public company who is also the owner of a small holding in the company's shares, it is easy to see the distinction between his interests as a managing director employed under service contract and his interests as a member. In the case of a small private company in which two or three members have invested their capital by subscribing for shares on the footing that dividends are unlikely but that each will earn his living by working for the company as a director, the distinction may be more elusive. The member's interests as a member who has ventured his capital in the company's business may include a legitimate expectation that he will continue to be employed as a director and his dismissal from that office and exclusion from the management of the company may therefore be unfairly prejudicial to his interests as a member.

[44] Gower's *Principles of Modern Company Law* (4th ed.), p. 669. But Lord Cross in *Re Westbourne Galleries* had endorsed the restrictive application of s. 210: [1973] A.C. 360, 385G–H.

> I bear in mind that Lord Wilberforce added that in most companies and in most contexts, whether the company was large or small, the member's rights under the articles of association and the Companies Act could be treated as an exhaustive statement of his interests as a member. He mentioned various features typically present in cases in which further equitable considerations might arise: a personal relationship between shareholders involving mutual confidence, an agreement that some or all should participate in the management and restrictions on the transfer of shares which would prevent a member from realising his investment."[45]

4–028 A very wide application of the concept of the "rights, expectations and obligations" of a shareholder was contemplated by the same judge in *Re A Company (No. 003160 of 1986)*.[46] In that case, a husband was a joint venturer in a company, but for various reasons his shares were temporarily registered in his wife's name. The husband having been discharged as an employee, he and his wife were faced with the apparent difficulty that, on the one hand, he was not registered as a shareholder and therefore had no *locus standi* to present a petition,[47] and on the other hand, she had taken no real part in the establishment or running of the joint venture. Hoffmann J. doubted whether this was a real difficulty: see the passage in his judgment cited at paragraph 4–009, above.

4–029 As appears from the passage cited at paragraph 4–027 above, there will be many cases where the rights of members are limited to their strict legal rights stated in the articles of association of the company or elsewhere. In *Re Blue Arrow plc*[48] the petitioner complained about being removed from her position as non-executive president of the company. The company had been floated on the Unlisted Securities Market. Vinelott J. held that it was impossible to infer that any legitimate expectation to remain president arose in favour of the petitioner from arrangements outside the formal constitution of the company:

> "Outside investors were entitled to assume that the whole of the constitution was contained in the articles, read, of course, with the Companies Acts."[49]

To similar effect is the decision of Hoffmann J. in *Re Posgate & Denby (Agencies) Ltd.*[50] In that case, the non-voting equity shareholders alleged

[45] [1986] B.C.L.C. 376, 378g–379f. (1986) B.C.C. 99,171.
[46] [1986] B.C.L.C. 391
[47] See para. 4–007 above.
[48] [1987] B.C.L.C. 585.
[49] At p. 590g–h.
[50] [1987] B.C.L.C. 8.

that their interests were being prejudiced by the proposal of the directors and holders of the voting shares to sell parts of the business to themselves without the approval of the equity shareholders. The articles of association and the provisions of the Companies Acts in relation to conflicts of interest had been satisfied, and no allegation of breach of fiduciary duty was made. Hoffmann J. held that there were no equitable considerations which extended the interests of the equity shareholders beyond their rights contained in the articles. The articles expressly contemplated conflicts of interest on the part of directors and the exclusion of equity shareholders from voting notwithstanding their interest in the company, so that it was "impossible to superimpose an obligation of fairness"[51] requiring the approval of the equity shareholders to the proposed sales.

4–030 Upon the authority of *Re Posgate & Denby (Agencies) Ltd.* (*supra*) it may be said that, unless there are special circumstances present, for example, in small private companies formed as joint ventures between a group of persons on the basis of mutual trust and confidence, the courts will be very reluctant to extend the rights of members beyond those stated expressly in the constitution of the company. If the position were otherwise, it might be argued that the courts were arrogating to themselves the right to interfere in contractual and commercial arrangements wherever fairness required such intervention.[52]

(2) *Part of the Members*

4–031 If the remedy under Part XVII of the 1985 Act were seen solely as a remedy to protect minorities against the unacceptable face of majority rule, then it would be central to the statutory test of unfair prejudice that there exists the element of discrimination against the petitioning shareholder, alone or amongst other shareholders, or in other words that he is not being treated equally to other shareholders. If all shareholders are equally prejudiced, then there cannot exist any relevant minority or any grievance shared by any such minority.

4–032 Given that discrimination will usually involve unfairness, clearly the element of discrimination may be relevant to a finding of unfair prejudice. More significantly, the requirement that the prejudiced interests be those of "some part" of the members would appear to lead to the conclusion that there can be no unfair prejudice if all of the members are equally prejudiced. There is substantial judicial support for this conclusion.[53] In *Re A Company (No. 00370 of 1987) ex p. Glossop* Harman J. held:

[51] At p. 14i.
[52] See *Re Ringtower Holdings plc* (1989) 5 B.C.C. 82, 94.
[53] See also *Carrington* v. *Viyella* (1983) B.C.C. 98,951, 98,959.

> "It may be regrettable but, in my view, the statute providing a statutory remedy, although in wide terms in part, does contain the essential provision that the conduct complained of must be conduct unfairly prejudicial to some part of the members, and that cannot possibly mean unfairly prejudicial to all of the members. The phrase 'some part of the members,' where it occurs, points, in my judgment, beyond any question, to a distinction between the part and the whole. In my view Parliament has provided something which affects—to use a different word—a slice of the members, whether it be a chunk out of a pie chart or however one envisages a slice. I am of opinion that no sec. 459 petition could be based upon conduct that has an equal effect on all the shareholders and was not intended to be discriminatory between shareholders."[54]

This reasoning was, however, rejected by Peter Gibson J. in *Re Sam Weller & Sons Ltd.*[55] The learned judge held that it was undesirable to put any gloss, such as the element of discrimination, on the language of the statute. He noted that Harman J.'s test overlooked the extended meaning of the interests of members, which was not limited to their interests as members, and the element of unfairness, which made it possible that the interests of only some members might be unfairly prejudiced even though all the members were prejudiced by the conduct complained of. Peter Gibson J. referred, in particular, to *Scottish Co-op Wholesale Society* v. *Meyer*[56] as an example of a case where there is unfair prejudice to the interests of some part of the members, even though, *qua* members of the company, those responsible have suffered an equal or greater prejudice.

There are cases where it is difficult to identify any element of discrimination against particular shareholders, no matter how elastic a view is taken of their "interests," yet there is no good reason to exclude the jurisdiction of the court on that ground alone. In *Ex p. McGuinness,*[57] the petitioner's complaint was that the directors, having received a members requisition to convene an E.G.M. to change the constitution of the board, had for no good reason convened an E.G.M. for a date far in the future. Lord Davidson, in the Court of Session (Outer House), held that the petitioner had established unfair prejudice to his interests. There does not appear to have been any argument on, nor did Lord Davidson consider, the point whether there had been inequality of treatment amongst shareholders.

[54] (1988) 4 B.C.C. 507, 511; [1988] 1 W.L.R. 1068.
[55] (1989) 5 B.C.C. 810.
[56] [1959] A.C. 324.
[57] (1988) 4 B.C.C. 161.

(3) *Prejudice*

4–033 The variety of ways in which prejudice may be suffered by members is almost unlimited. Clearly, prejudice includes cases where "the value of his shareholding in the company has been seriously diminished or at least seriously jeopardised."[58] A classic and extreme example of such diminution in value is provided by the facts of *Scottish Co-op Wholsesale Society* v. *Meyer* (*supra*), where the majority shareholders had pursued a policy of running down the business of the company to the benefit of their own competing business, thereby drastically reducing the value of the shares in the company.

Another common example is that of a small private company formed as a quasi-partnership in which the joint venturers expect to share in the business by reason of their continued employment therein. If that employment is terminated, then clearly the interests of that joint venturer have been prejudiced. In such a case, however, prejudice is obviously suffered, even though there is no effect on the value of shares. This, of course, must follow from the elastic meaning given to the interests of members and the inclusion of interests other than as members.

Conversely, in cases where the only relevant interests are those as shareholders, prejudice may be suffered despite the absence of any effect on the value of any shares. Thus, in *Ex p. McGuinness* (*supra*) it was held that the unreasonable delay in convening a meeting upon receipt of a member's requisition constituted prejudice, since "justice delayed is justice denied" and "delay is prejudicial to the interests of a person who seeks to work out a legal remedy."[59]

4–034 Even if the court will accept prejudice short of demonstrable financial loss, it will not accept prejudice of a speculative or vague nature. In *Re A Company (No. 001761 of 1986)*[60] it was argued by the petitioner that he had suffered prejudice as a shareholder, because his joint-venturer had, without informing the petitioner, arguably acquired an advantage by paying off the bank mortgagee and stepping into its shoes. Harman J. held[61] that the company (and, hence, its members) had not been prejudiced, since its position had not changed in any way.

[58] *Per* Slade L.J. in *Re Bovey Hotel Ventures Ltd.*, unreported, C.A. July 31, 1981, but referred to in *Re R.A. Noble (Clothing) Ltd.* (1983) B.C.L.C. 273. See also *Re A Company (No. 00789 of 1987)* (1989) 5 B.C.C. 792. In that case Harman J. held that the failure to conduct the affairs of a company properly from a procedural point of view could amount to unfair prejudice where the improprieties resulted in the invalidity of an allotment of shares to the petitioner: at pp.800, 801.
[59] (1988) 4 B.C.C. 161, at p. 167.
[60] [1987] B.C.L.C. 141.
[61] At p. 147.

(4) *Unfairness*

4–035 As Peter Gibson J. held in *Re Ringtower Holdings plc*[62]:

> " . . . (2) the [relevant] conduct must be both prejudicial . . . to the relevant interests and also unfairly so: conduct may be unfair without being prejudicial or prejudicial without being unfair and in neither case could the section be satisfied;
> (3) the test is of unfair prejudice, not of unlawfulness, and conduct may be lawful but unfairly prejudical . . . "

Whilst it is, therefore, essential that the relevant prejudice has been caused unfairly, the test of fairness is an extremely wide one and allows the court to have regard to any circumstances that it considers to be relevant. Save by reference to decided cases, it is difficult to predict how the court will exercise its discretion in this context. For example, the court can take into account any of the following factors:

(1) Any misconduct on the part of the petitioner.[63]
(2) Any alternative remedy available to the petitioner.[64]
(3) Any offer made to the petitioner.[65]
(4) The motives of those in control of the company.[66]
(5) Any delay in presenting the petition.[67]

Applications of Unfair Prejudice Test

Exclusion from Management

4–036 In the early days of the unfair prejudice remedy, it was still a matter of argument whether, in the case of a quasi-partnership where the quasi-partners expect to participate in management, in other words the type of company considered in *Re Westbourne Galleries*, a member could complain about exclusion from management: see *Re A Company (No. 002567 of 1982)*.[68] In *Re R. A. Noble (Clothing) Ltd.*,[69] however, Nourse J. held that a course of conduct resulting in "the exclusion of [a joint venturer] from

[62] (1989) 5 B.C.C. 82, 90.
[63] See the discussions below of (1) exclusion from management and (2) diversion of business, respectively; *Re Noble & Sons (Clothing) Ltd.* [1983] B.C.L.C. 273; *Re London School of Electronics* [1986] Ch. 211.
[64] See the discussions below of (1) pre-emption articles and (2) alternative remedies, respectively.
[65] See the discussion below of reasonable offers.
[66] See the discussion below of improper purposes.
[67] See *D.R. Chemicals Ltd.* (1989) 5 B.C.C. 39.
[68] [1983] B.C.L.C. 151, 158d.
[69] [1983] B.C.L.C. 273, 291h.

participation in all major decisions affecting the Company's affairs" amounted to conduct prejudicial to the interests of the joint venturer. In *Re A Company (No. 00477 of 1986)*, Hoffmann J. endorsed this trend by holding that a joint venturer might have a legitimate expectation as a member to be employed by the company as a director.[70] To the same effect are the judgments of the same judge in *Re A Company (No. 007623 of 1984)*,[71] *Re A Company (No. 003160 of 1986)*,[72] and *Re XYZ Ltd.*[73]

It is clear,[74] therefore, that in the case of a quasi-partnership it may be part of the legitimate expectations of a member as such to be involved in the management of a company, and in particular to be employed with a salary. One of the reasons for the recognition of this expectation is a fiscal one, namely that there used to be a taxation advantage in extracting profits from a company in the form of earned income as salary rather than as unearned income as dividend. This tax advantage no longer applies.[75] Participation in the profits of a company need, therefore, no longer be so closely linked with participation in the management of the company.

4–037 Two different approaches to the application of the unfair prejudice test to cases of exclusion from management have appeared from the authorities. In *Re R.A. Noble & Sons (Clothing) Ltd. (supra)*[76] the essence of the allegation of unfair prejudice was that one joint-venturer had been excluded from involvement in the major decisions of the company. Nourse J. considered the lengthy and detailed evidence. He observed: " . . . it seems to me that [the two joint venturers] is each in part the author of his own misfortunes. This is not, as will appear, to say that they were equally to blame, but each must bear a share of the blame for what happened".[77] He concluded:

> " . . . I do not think that it can be said that [the Respondent's] conduct was unfairly prejudicial to the interests of [the Petitioner]. In my judgment, the crucial word on the facts of this case is 'unfairly.' It is at this point that [the Petitioner's] disinterest becomes a decisive factor. In the end, . . . I do not think that a reasonable bystander, observing the consequences of [the Respondent's] conduct and

[70] See [1986] B.C.L.C. 376. at pp. 379h–390a, and passage at pp. 378g–379f cited at para. 4–027, above.

[71] [1986] B.C.L.C. 362; (1986) 2 B.C.C. 99,191.

[72] [1986] B.C.L.C. 391; (1986) 2 B.C.C. 99,276.

[73] [1987] 1 W.L.R. 102.

[74] See also *Re A Company (No. 003096 of 1987)* (1988) 4 B.C.C. 80; *Re D.R. Chemicals Ltd.* (1989) 5 B.C.C. 39.

[75] *Per* Harman J. in *Re A Company (No. 00370 of 1987)* (1988) 4 B.C.C. 507, 511–512; [1988] 1 W.L.R. 1068.

[76] See also the similar approach of the same judge in *Re Bird Precision Bellows* [1984] Ch. 419 (in C.A.: [1986] Ch. 658; *Re London School of Electronics* [1986] Ch. 211.

[77] [1983] B.C.L.C. 273, at pp. 288i–289a.

judging it to have been prejudicial to the interests of [the Petitioner], would regard it as having been unfair. I think he would say that [the Petitioner] had partly brought it upon himself. That means that there is no case for relief under section 75."[78]

In other words, upon the authority of this decision, it is generally necessary, in the case of a breakdown of relations between joint venturers and the exclusion of one from the business, to analyse the evidence in detail and decide whether the excluded party was partly to blame for the result. If so, there was no unfair prejudice to him.[79]

4-038 In contrast, in *Re A Company (No. 007623 of 1984)*,[80] Hoffmann J., on similar facts, rejected the petitioner's argument that the exclusion of a joint venturer from the business necessarily amounted to unfair prejudice unless his conduct "plainly justified" his exclusion. The learned judge held:

> "I think that this reasoning oversimplifies the realities of a business relationship. There are many cases in which it becomes in practice impossible for two people to work together without obvious fault on either side. They may have come together with a confident expectation of being able to co-operate but found that insurmountable differences in personality made it impossible. In those circumstances the only solution is for them to part company. If one of them asks the other to leave the business, I cannot accept that the former must automatically be regarded as having acted in a manner unfairly prejudicial to the interests of the latter. It must depend on whether it is reasonable that one should leave rather than the other and, even more important, on the terms on which he is asked to go. In this case it seems clear to me that, without apportioning any blame, the petitioner's departure was a reasonable way of dealing with the breakdown in relations between himself and his nephew. The petitioner was in a minority; he was an employee rather than an entrepreneur and he was nearly sixty years old. There was never any suggestion from him that he should take over the company."[81]

Thus, upon the authority of this decision,[82] unless there is "obvious fault" on the part of one side, the court will not attempt to investigate where the blame for the breakdown lies, but will rather consider the practicalities of the situation and the reasonableness of the treatment of the excluded

[78] At p.292a–b.

[79] The learned judge went on to hold, however, that the same facts justified winding-up order.

[80] [1986] B.C.L.C. 362; (1986) 2 B.C.C. 99,191.

[81] At p. 366a–d.

[82] This decision was cited with approval by the same judge in *Re XYZ Ltd.* [1987] 1 W.L.R. 102 and by Peter Gibson J. in *Re A Company (No 003096 of 1987)* (1988) 4 B.C.C. 80.

party. In most cases,[83] the effect of this decision will be that the excluded party is entitled to have his shares purchased at a fair value, even if he is partly to blame for his expulsion.[84]

4–039 It is only, however, in certain circumstances that a shareholder will have any legitimate expectation to be involved in the management of the company. The classic example where such an expectation may arise is that of the so-called "quasi-partnership" which has one or more of the following ingredients:

> "The superimposition of equitable considerations requires something more, which typically may include one, or probably more, of the following elements: (i) an association formed or continued on the basis of a personal relationship, involving mutual confidence—this element will often be found where a pre-existing partnership has been converted into a limited company; (ii) an agreement, or understanding, that all, or some (for there may be 'sleeping' members), of the shareholders shall participate in the conduct of the business; (iii) restriction upon the transfer of the members' interest in the company—so that if confidence is lost, or one member is removed from management, he cannot take out his stake and go elsewhere."[85]

To take an extreme example, a shareholder in a quoted public company obviously has no legitimate expectation without more to participate in management. Furthermore, even in the case of small private companies, the joint venturers may have concluded detailed agreements which contemplate, *inter alia*, one party excluding the other from management. In such cases,[86] the court is likely to hold that these agreements are exhaustive of the rights of the parties and there is no room for the superimposition of any equitable rights to management participation.

Diversion of Business

4–040 It is clear that the deliberate diversion of the company's business by those in control of the company to another business owned by them is capable of amounting to unfair prejudice of the shareholders who have no

[83] But see discussion of pre-emption articles below. Also, see discussion of share valuation and *Re Bird Precision Bellows Ltd.* [1984] Ch. 419, 430G–431C.

[84] See the further judgment of Hoffmann J. in *Re A Company (No. 006834 of 1988)* (1989) 5 B.C.C. 218, discussed at para. 4–060 below.

[85] *Per* Lord Wilberforce in *Re Westbourne Galleries Ltd.* [1973] A.C. 360, 379. See at para. 3–018 above.

[86] See *Re XYZ Ltd.* (1987) 1 W.L.R. 102, *Re A Company (No. 003096 of 1987)* (1988) 4 B.C.C. 80, and *Re Ringtower Holdings plc* (1989) 5 B.C.C. 82.

interest in the new business.[87] This is another classic example of conduct which excludes the minority from full participation in the profits of the company. Furthermore, as Slade L.J. noted in *Re Bovey Hotel Ventures Ltd.*,[88] it is not necessary to show that those in control had acted in bad faith, for it is sufficient if a reasonable bystander would regard the consequences of their conduct as having unfairly prejudiced the petitioner's interests.

Excessive Remuneration

4–041 The payment of excessive remuneration to directors, to the detriment of the members, was one of the examples of conduct which the Cohen Committee[89] cited in favour of the enactment of section 210 of the 1948 Act. It is clear that, if the controlling directors pay themselves remuneration not by reference to a proper reward for services rendered but as a disguised payment of dividend, then such conduct would be unfairly prejudicial to the interests of those members who were not directors.[90] In *Re Jermyn St. Turkish Baths*,[91] a case concerned with section 210 of the 1948 Act, excessive remuneration was referred to as "such [as] was grossly in excess of any reasonable return for their services in conducting the affairs of the company."

4–042 Unless it can be shown that the directors have pursued a deliberate policy of not paying dividends and instead paying salaries related to profits rather than services rendered, it will be difficult in practice in most cases to prove that the remuneration paid was excessive. The courts have a natural disinclination to find remuneration excessive. In *Smith* v. *Croft*,[92] a derivative action alleging breach of fiduciary duty, Walton J. rejected, in forthright language, the plaintiff's contention that the directors' salaries were excessive and warned that in certain areas of business, such as the entertainment business, salaries were justifiable though far in excess of what could be earned in other professions. The courts will not generally interfere with matters which require the commercial judgement of the board. Thus, in general, if the board has honestly and genuinely exercised the power to pay remuneration, the court will not determine whether the remuneration awarded was reasonable.[93]

[87] See *Scottish Co-operative Wholesale* v. *Meyer* [1959] A.C. 324 ; *Re Stewarts (Brixton) Ltd.* [1985] B.C.L.C. 4; *Re London School of Electronics* [1986] Ch. 211; *Re XYZ Ltd.* [1987] 1 W.L.R. 102; *Re Cumana* (1986) B.C.C. 99,453, [1986] B.C.L.C. 430 (C.A.).
[88] See n. 58 above.
[89] Cmd. 6659, paras. 58 and 59.
[90] See *Re A Company (No. 004377 of 1986)* [1987] B.C.L.C. 94, 99i.
[91] [1971] 1 W.L.R. 1042, 1059E.
[92] (1986) 2 B.C.C. 99,010, 99,019; [1986] 1 W.L.R. 580.
[93] See *Re Halt Garages Ltd.* [1982] 3 All E.R. 1016.

Nevertheless, the unfair prejudice remedy obliges the court to consider the reasonableness of the remuneration in question. In *Re Cumana*[94] the court found that remuneration paid was excessive. In that case, the respondent was alleged to have received in the region of £160,000 to £356,000 by way of bonus and £190,000 by way of pension contributions.[95] Vinelott J. concluded:

> "The remuneration paid to [the Respondent] . . . was plainly in excess of anything he had earned and was so large as to be unfairly prejudicial to [the Petitioner]."[96]

Inadequate Dividends

4–043 The failure to pay adequate dividends, coupled with the payment of excessive remuneration, will sometimes form the basis of an allegation of unfair prejudice. There is no longer any general tax advantage in distributing profits in the guise of remuneration rather than dividends, so there is a greater incentive to pay dividends. In *Re A Company (No. 00370 of 1987) ex p. Glossop*,[97] however, Harman J. held that it was not enough for a petitioner to allege that the directors, whilst continuing to draw remuneration, had failed to repay reasonable dividends out of the substantial profits. The company was a small private business run by the petitioner's late husband prior to his death. The basis of Harman J.'s judgment is set out in the passage cited at paragraph 4–032 above. In essence, Harman J. held that the conduct complained of was not discriminatory between shareholders.[98] The learned judge went on, however, to hold that failure to pay dividends could be grounds for winding up the company on the just and equitable ground.[99]

In *Re Sam Weller & Sons Ltd.*,[1] on the other hand, Peter Gibson J. declined to follow the above decision of Harman J. and held that the failure of the majority shareholders to pay reasonable dividends, whilst continuing to draw directors' fees and to accumulate reserves, could amount to conduct unfairly prejudicial to the interests of the minority

[94] (1986) 2 B.C.C. 99,453; [1986] B.C.L.C. 430 (C.A.).
[95] See at p. 99,460, column 2.
[96] At p. 99,482. The Court of Appeal agreed: [1986] B.C.L.C. 430, 435d–e.
[97] (1988) 4.B.C.C. 507; [1988] 1 W.L.R. 1068.
[98] It is arguable that the learned judge took too narrow a view of the interests of members and should have held that the non-director shareholders formed a separate class. See now *Re Sam Weller & Sons Ltd.* para. 4–032 above.
[99] For another case where the court held, in different circumstances, that winding up was the appropriate remedy, see *Re Noble & Sons (Clothing) Ltd.* (*supra*). See also para. 3–028 above.
[1] See para. 4–032 above.

shareholders. The learned judge did note, however, that the court would view with great caution allegations of unfair prejudice on this ground. This case was an extreme case where the directors had refused to consider the declaration of a dividend related to results. No doubt if a board gave bona fide consideration to the declaration of a dividend the court would not interfere with its commercial decision save in special circumstances.

Take-over Bids

4–044 In *Re A Company (No. 008699 of 1985)*[2] there were two rival bids for the shares in a private company: one from a company owned by the directors, another (the higher bid) from a third party. The directors had the ability to thwart the third party's bid by refusing to effect the necessary alterations to the articles and sent a circular to members urging them to accept their own, lower, bid. Some of the shareholders presented a petition on the unfair prejudice ground. Hoffmann J. rejected arguments that the petitioners' interests had not been prejudiced. He went on to hold that the contents of the circular could give rise to a claim of unfair prejudice:

> "Whether or not the board of a company faced with competing bids is under a positive duty to advise the shareholders to accept the higher offer, I think that if the board choose to give advice on the matter, fairness requires that such advice should be factually accurate and given with a view to enabling the shareholders . . . to sell, if they so wish, at the best price."[3]

Improper Purposes

4–045 Many types of conduct will be unfairly prejudicial if the purpose or effect thereof is discriminatory in some way between shareholders but will not be so if those concerned have made a bona fide commercial decision in the interests of the company. A typical example is that of a rights issue. On the one hand, a rights issue is a common means of raising capital from shareholders equally without diluting any shareholder's interest in the company. On the other hand, a rights issue may be discriminatory in certain circumstances. Thus, in *Re Cumana*, Vinelott J. held that the real purpose of a proposed rights issue was to embarrass the petitioner in his litigation against the respondent and to dilute the petitioner's interest.[4]

[2] [1986] B.C.L.C. 382; (1986) B.C.C. 99,024.

[3] At p. 388c–d. See also, on fiduciary duties of directors, *Heron International* v. *Grade* [1983] B.C.L.C. 244; *Dawson* v. *Coats Paton* [1989] B.C.L.C. 233; para. 5–21 below.

[4] (1986) 2 B.C.C. 99,453. See at pp. 99,480 and 99,482. For an even more blatant case of intention to dilute a member's interest, see *D.R. Chemicals Ltd.* (1989) 5 B.C.C. 39.

4–046 In contrast, in *Re A Company (No. 007623 of 1984)*,[5] the petitioner complained, *inter alia*, of a proposed rights issue which he did not have the resources to take up. Hoffmann J. found that the directors were acting reasonably in what they considered to be the interests of the company. He went on, however, to hold that the proposed rights issue was still capable of amounting to unfair prejudice:

> "Nevertheless, I do not think that the bona fides of the decision or the fact that the petitioner was offered shares on the same terms as other shareholders necessarily means that the rights issue could not have been unfairly prejudicial to his interests. If the majority know that the petitioner does not have the money to take up his rights and the offer is made at par when the shares are plainly worth a great deal more than par as part of a majority holding (but very little as a minority holding), it seems to me arguable that carrying through the transaction in that form could, viewed objectively, constitute unfairly prejudicial conduct. In this case, however, it seems to me that the petitioner, if he lacks the resources or inclination to contribute *pari passu* to the company, could protect his interests by offering to sell his existing holding to the majority. Indeed, if the company needs funds and he does not want to pay his share, it seems to me only fair that he should offer to sell out."[6]

It would appear, therefore, that there would have been no unfair prejudice if the subscription of the new shares reflected their true value.

Pre-emption Articles

4–047 A company's articles of association may contain a pre-emption provision, commonly that a shareholder desirous of transferring his shares is bound to offer to sell his shares to his co-shareholders at a fair value fixed by the auditors. In a series of first instance decisions concerning applications to strike out petitions, great weight has been placed on the presence of such a provision, but this is a developing area of the law.[6a]

The first reported such case was *Re A Company (No. 007623 of 1984)*. As noted above,[7] Hoffmann J. held that the proposed rights issue was capable of amounting to unfair prejudice. He went on to hold that the petitioner was nevertheless bound to invoke the pre-emption provisions in the company's articles:

> "In general it seems to me that if a petitioner is complaining of conduct which would be unfairly prejudicial only if accompanied by a

[5] [1986] B.C.L.C. 362.
[6] At p. 367a–c.
[6a] See para. 4–054 below.
[7] At para. 4–046 above.

refusal on the part of the majority to buy his shares at a fair price, and the articles provide a mechanism for determining such a price, he should not be entitled to petition under s.75 [of the 1980 Act] until he has invoked or offered to invoke that mechanism and the majority have refused to buy at the price so determined. Certification by the auditors is a swift and inexpensive method of arriving at a price and it has the merit of being the method to which the parties are contractually bound. Where such machinery is available, it seems to me wrong for a shareholder to insist on the same valuation exercise being undertaken by the court at far greater expense.

. . .

In the typical case in which (1) relations between shareholders have broken down without obvious fault on either side (2) the appropriate way to resolve the problem is for one or more shareholders to buy the shares of the other or others and (3) the company's articles provide a means for determining the fair value of those shares, it should not be necessary to resort to s.75 unless and until the operation of the articles has failed to provide an adequate solution."[8]

On the face of this passage, it would appear that in most cases where a share purchase order is the obvious remedy and there are pre-emption provisions, then no unfair prejudice petition will lie until those provisions have been exhausted.

4–048 The learned judge restated that rule, whilst also adding some qualifications thereto, in *Re XYZ Ltd.*[9] That was a case where the pre-emption provisions, unusually, expressly required a shareholder ceasing to be a director or employee of the company to give a transfer notice, and the learned judge held that there was no room for any equitable gloss on this provision. The learned judge went on, however, to deal with the usual case of a breakdown in relations between joint venturers and repeated the general rule.[10]

He noted the following qualifications:

"I must emphasis that there is no allegation in the petition of any wrongful conduct by the board or majority shareholders in the way that they have run or are running the company. There is no suggestion that they are paying themselves excessive salaries, diverting business to other companies or doing any of the things frequently alleged to constitute unfairly prejudicial conduct.

. . .

I say nothing about cases in which there has been bad faith or plain impropriety in the conduct of the respondents or about cases in

[8] [1986] B.C.L.C. 362, at pp. 367g–h, and 368a–b.
[9] [1987] B.C.L.C. 94; [1987] 1 W.L.R. 102.
[10] At p. 102a–b.

which the articles provide some arbitrary or artificial method of valuation."[11]

It would appear that the reason for the exclusion of cases such as the payment of excessive salaries is that the auditors, under the pre-emption provisions, would be bound to fix a value as at the present and would be unable to make allowance for unfairly prejudicial conduct. No such difficulty arises in the case of exclusion from management upon a breakdown of relations.

4–049 For a number of reasons, in certain circumstances, the application of the above rule may be unsatisfactory[12]:

(1) It appears wrong in principle to deny a joint venturer a determination of the responsibility for the breakdown in relations because of the difficulty of that determination. It should be irrelevant, for example, that the petitioner is legally aided.
(2) Pre-emption provisions, in their usual form, do not make express provision for a shareholder ceasing to be a director but rather for a shareholder being desirous of transferring his shares. Without a determination of the responsibility for the breakdown of relations, how can it be said that the petitioner is so desirous? If, in reality, he is not, the application of the pre-emption provisions is, in effect, an arbitrary attempt to stem the floodgates of litigation.
(3) In practice, the auditors will often be closely involved with the respondents and will in any event have to continue to work with them in the future. Whilst auditors are, of course, professional accountants, in small private companies the petitioner may have an understandable lack of confidence in their impartiality.
(4) The auditor will invariably apply a discount for a minority shareholding in fixing a fair value under pre-emption provisions unless they preclude the application of such a discount, whereas it may not always be fair to apply such a discount depending on the circumstances.

4–050 These factors have not, however, carried weight with the courts. This issue was considered by Morritt J. in *Re Boswell (Steels) & Co. Ltd.*[13] In

[11] At pp. 99j and 102b.
[12] It is arguable that this general rule is inconsistent with the decision of the Court of Appeal in *Re Bird Precision Bellows Ltd.* [1986] Ch. 658. It is clear from the judgment of Oliver L.J. that the court was concerned with whether unfair prejudice had been established (see p. 501c–d), yet no one suggested that the company's articles, which contained a pre-emption provision in a common form (see p. 504e), were relevant to the issue of unfair prejudice. This decision is distinguished in *Re Castleburn* and *Re A Company (No. 006834 of 1988)*, which are discussed at paras. 4–052 to 4–053 below. See also para. 4–054 below.
[13] (1989) 5 B.C.C. 145.

that case, a minority shareholder with no legitimate expectation of management participation complained about the transfer of the business of a company to another company controlled by the minority shareholders and presented a petition on the unfair prejudice ground, alternatively to wind up. The Company's articles contained common-form rights of pre-emption whereby the auditor would value the shares. The majority shareholders offered to buy the petitioner's shares under the procedure contained in the articles. The petitioner objected to this offer on the grounds, *inter alia*, that the auditor might apply a discount for a minority shareholding, whereas the petitioner claimed there should be no discount, and that it was not appropriate for the auditor to investigate allegations of misfeasance. These objections were rejected by the learned judge. After quoting with approval from the judgment of Hoffmann J. in *Re XYZ Ltd.*,[14] he held:

> "(T)he question of what, if any, discount should be applied may quite fairly and reasonably be left to the valuer. Equally, the effect of misfeasance claims the company may have against its directors and others may in any given case also be left to the valuer, if he is truly independent."[15]

4–051 The learned judge, however, allowed the petition to continue on another ground, namely that it was not a case where the auditor " . . . was, and would be seen to be, wholly independent of any of the respondents and to have no connection with the transactions of which complaint was made."[16] In that case, the auditor had given advice to the directors at the time of the allegedly unfairly prejudicial transfer of the business and had sworn an affidavit which appeared to prejudge the issues raised in the petition.

4–052 In *Re Castleburn Ltd.*[17] the company was a quasi-partnership where the minority shareholder had been removed as a director as a result of a breakdown of relations. The articles of association contained common-form rights of pre-emption and the majority shareholders offered to buy the minority's shares at the value certified by the auditors. The minority presented an unfair prejudice petition, and objected to the majority's offer on the ground that the auditor had applied a discount for minority shareholding. Judge Baker, Q.C. struck the petition out. This case is remarkable for the fact that the petitioner did not rely on the fact that the company was a quasi-partnership.[18]

[14] Para. 4–048 above.
[15] At pp. 150H–151A.
[16] At p. 151A–B.
[17] (1989) 5 B.C.C. 652
[18] At pp. 660H–661E.

The learned judge first emphasised that the only dispute in the case was over the terms on which the respondent should buy out the petitioner: there were no allegations of wrongful conduct on the part of the respondents, such as the payment of excessive salaries or the diversion of business.[19] The petitioner's principal submission, namely that the auditors' valuation disclosed a fundamental error, was rejected, although the learned judge indicated that this submission could be pursued by way of an ordinary action against the auditors which would disclose a cause of action.[20] The petitioner relied on *Re Bird Precision Bellows,*[21] but the learned judge distinguished that decision on the grounds that the wording of the pre-emption article in that case was significantly different. The learned judge concluded by holding that the case before him fell squarely within the principles stated by Hoffmann J. in *Re XYZ Ltd.*[22]

4–053 The reasoning in *Re XYZ Ltd.* was applied by Hoffmann J. again in *Re A Company (No. 006834 of 1988)*.[23] In this case, the facts were similar to *Re Castleburn (supra)*, save that the majority offered to buy the minority's shares at their "open market value" to be determined by an independent valuer. The minority rejected this offer and presented an unfair prejudice petition. The important judgment of Hoffmann J. is discussed in the interest of reasonable offers at paragraph 4–060 below.

4–054 In contrast, in *Re Abbey Leisure Ltd.*, [23a] the Court of Appeal declined to strike out a winding-up petition on the just and equitable ground, in circumstances similar to the above first instance cases, except that it was a crucial factor that the company's principal asset was cash. It was this factor which caused the Court of Appeal to conclude that, for the purposes of section 125(2) of the 1986 Act, [24] the petitioner was not being unreasonable [24a] in "refusing to accept the risk of a discount being applied to the valuation of his interest in the Company" by an independent accountant. Balcambe L.J. also observed that, since the pre-emption article was subject to equitable considerations on *Re Westbourne Galleries* principles,[25] it was not an appropriate case for striking out. It has yet to be seen whether this decision of the Court of Appeal undermines the reasoning of the abovc first instance decisions.

[19] At p. 654B.
[20] At p. 660E.
[21] [1986] Ch. 658.
[22] [1987] B.C.L.C. 94.
[23] (1989) 5 B.C.C. 218.
[23a] November 21, 1989. Overruling (1989) 5 B.C.C. 183.
[24] See para. 3–001 above.
[24a] The Court of Appeal held that it was free to reach its own conclusion on this issue.
[25] See para. 3–018 above.

Reasonable Offers

4–055 If the petitioner seeks an order that his shares be purchased at a price fixed by the court, and the respondents offer to buy his shares at a reasonable price to be fixed by an independent valuer, then the court will in general stay or strike out the petition.[26]

4–056 The same reasoning applies in the case of a winding-up petition on the just and equitable ground. If a petitioner is seeking the winding-up of the company and he is offered the equivalent of the amount that he would receive by way of distribution in the winding-up, then it is clear that the petition will not be allowed to proceed. That offer will take the form of an offer to buy the petitioner's shares at a value equal to that amount.

4–057 In *Re A Company (No. 002567 of 1982)*[27] the petitioner was a quasi-partner who had been excluded from management and who apparently had an unassailable right to a winding-up order. His quasi-partners made offers to purchase his shares and the offer was ultimately refined to one whereby they agreed to buy the shares at a value to be determined by an independent valuer, who would value the petitioner's one-third shareholding at one third of the value of the company's net assets.[28] The petitioner rejected this offer for two principal reasons:

(1) the value of the company's assets could only be ascertained by an actual sale by a liquidator, either as a going concern or on a break-up basis[29];
(2) a liquidator could investigate whether there had been any misfeasance.

So far as the first reason was concerned, Vinelott J. held:

> "Whether if T [the petitioner] had made it clear in August 1980 that he was not willing to sell his shares at any price but would insist on a winding up of the company and had presented a petition forthwith, it would have been right to make a winding-up order notwithstanding the offer that has now been made, I do not find it necessary to decide. That is not what happened in this case. At the time when T was first excluded from participation in the affairs of the company he was willing to sell his shares to his co-shareholders if a fair price could be negotiated. Negotiations having proved unfruitful, his co-shareholders now offer to acquire his shares at a value reached by a machinery which, in my judgment, meets all T's reasonable objections. In insisting on a winding-up order he is, in effect, asking that

[26] *Re A Company (No. 003843 of 1986)* [1987] B.C.L.C. 562. But see para. 4–054.
[27] [1983] B.C.L.C. 151.
[28] See at p. 156g–h.
[29] See the partnership case of *Syers* v. *Syers* (1876) 1 App.Cas. 174.

the respondents should either buy out his shares at the price he chooses to place on them, or face the disruption of a winding-up order and that notwithstanding the fact that at least until July of 1982 they continued to run the company in the expectation that a price, or a fair machinery for ascertaining the price, could be agreed and exposed themselves to a continuing liability under a guarantee to the company's bankers to do so."[30]

So far as the second reason was concerned, Vinelott J. held that the valuer would have power to investigate and pursue any misfeasance, and in any event there was no evidence of any misfeasance.[31]

The learned judge went on to hold that, because he concluded that the petitioner had in the course of negotiations used the threat of a winding-up petition to extract an inflated value for his shares, the date of valuation should not be the date of his exclusion from management but the date of the submission to the valuer. He also ordered the petitioner to pay the costs of the petition, which was dismissed.

4–058 The above decision of Vinelott J. was applied in *Re A Company (No. 003843 of 1986)*.[32] In that case, the offer to buy the petitioners' one-half shareholding was one-half of the market value of the company as a going concern. Millett J. observed that this offer, if accepted, would result in the earlier payment of a greater sum to the petitioners than they would have achieved in a winding-up.[33]

4–059 In both of the preceding cases the respondents conceded that the petitioner's shares should be valued as fraction of the value of the entire issued share capital of the company. In cases concerning minority shareholdings, however, the majority may only wish to buy the minority's shares on the basis that the valuer either applies a discount for a minority shareholding or has a discretion whether to apply such a discount. In cases where the articles include pre-emption rights, it has been held at first instance[34] that the minority is bound to accept the discretion of the auditor, depending on the precise wording of the articles. It would further appear, by analogy with the authorities on pre-emption rights, that the minority cannot generally insist on the court investigating allegations of misfeasance against the majority: this is something that can be taken into account by the independent valuer.

4–060 If, however, the articles do not contain pre-emption provisions, it is arguable that it would generally be wrong in principle to subject a minority shareholder to the discretion of an independent valuer on the

[30] At p. 161d–g.
[31] See at p. 163. In *Re Abbey Leisure Ltd.* (C.A.), para. 4–054 above, it is suggested that the Court's powers may be superior.
[32] [1987] B.C.L.C. 562.
[33] At p. 571b–c. See also *Re A Company (No. 003096 of 1987)* (1988) 4 B.C.C. 80.
[34] See para. 4–050 above. But see para. 4–054 also.

issue of a discount for a minority shareholder, where it is arguable that no such discount should be applied.[35] There are, however, dicta in *Re A Company (No. 006834 of 1988)*[36] which suggest that a minority shareholder is not entitled to a judicial determination on that issue. The company was again a quasi-partnership, where the articles contained common-form rights of pre-emption. There was a breakdown of relations, and the majority offered to buy the minority's shares at their "open market value" to be determined by an independent valuer. Under the articles, the value was the "fair value" determined by the auditor. The minority presented a petition on the unfair prejudice ground. Hoffmann J. held that it was inconceivable that the court would order the majority to sell their shares to the minority. The question, therefore, was the value of the minority's shares. The learned judge held that the petition should be struck out. The learned judge observed:

> "The principle to be derived from the cases is that when it is plain that the appropriate solution to a breakdown of relations is for the petitioner to be able to sell his shares at a fair price and the articles contain provisions for determining a price which the respondent is willing to pay or the respondent has offered to submit to an independent determination of a fair price, the presentation or maintenance of a petition under sec. 459 will ordinarily be an abuse of the process: see *Re A Company No. 003096 of 1987* (1988) 4 B.C.C. 80, and the earlier cases therein referred to."[37]

It is noteworthy from this passage that the learned judge was not confining his remarks to companies which had pre-emption provisions. In his judgment, the position was the same if the majority made a fair offer for the minority's shares. The learned judge then observed:

> "This is an ordinary case of breakdown of confidence between the parties. In such circumstances, fairness requires that the minority shareholder should not have to maintain his investment in a company managed by the majority with whom he has fallen out."[38]

In other words, in cases of breakdown in confidence in the case of quasi-partnerships, the court will not need to determine the blame for the breakdown but will hold that the breakdown itself is sufficient to found an unfair prejudice petition (and presumably also a winding-up petition on the just and equitable ground). The learned judge then added, however, the following significant qualification:

> "But the unfairness disappears if the minority shareholder is offered a fair price for his shares. In such a case, sec. 459 was not intended to

[35] *Re Abbey Leisure Ltd.* (C.A.), para. 4–054 above. See also *Re D. R. Chemicals Ltd.* (1989) 5 B.C.C. 39, 53–54, and para. 4–066 below.
[36] (1989) 5 B.C.C. 218.
[37] At p. 220G–H.
[38] At p. 221C–D.

> enable the court to preside over a protracted and expensive contest of virtue between the shareholders and to award the company to the winner."

This passage appears to mean that, although it may be easier for a minority shareholder to present a petition, since he will not have to establish blame, he may not be able to insist on establishing blame so as to achieve a valuation of his shares on a non-discounted basis.

In respect of the petitioner objecting that there were allegations of misfeasance which required investigation, the learned judge held:

> "(T)here might be cases of impropriety on the part of the respondent which had so affected the value of the shares in the company as to make it inappropriate for the matter to be dealt with by a straightforward valuation. In this case, however, the effect of the alleged improprieties on the valuation of the shares in the company is likely to be minimal. What the valuer will be concerned with is applying a suitable multiple to the profits which the company appears to be likely to earn in the future. Furthermore, Mr. Kramer has said that the valuer should be free, if he felt it fair to do so, to write back into the accounts any sums which he considered to have been improperly disbursed."[39]

4–061 In respect of the petitioner's objection that the shares should be valued on a non-discounted basis, the learned judge rejected these objections and distinguished the case of *Re Bird Precision Bellows*.[40] It follows that a majority may be well advised to make an offer to buy the minority's shares on a basis that leaves it to the discretion of the valuer whether to apply a discount for a minority shareholding, rather than incur the cost and uncertainty of a trial in which the court might find that no discount should be applied.

4–062 One difficulty about *Re A Company (No. 006834 of 1988) (supra)* is that the majority's offer referred to the "open market value" of the shares, which the learned judge interpreted to mean that the "valuer is asked to determine a fair value, and it is left to him to decide whether to apply a discount or not."[41] An "open market" valuation is, however, generally regarded to be harsher to a minority shareholder than a "fair" valuation.[42]

4–063 It cannot be a sufficient answer to every unfair prejudice petition that the respondents are willing to buy the petitioner's shares at a fair value. For example, the petitioner may have an arguable case to buy out the

[39] At p. 221g–h.
[40] [1986] Ch. 658. It will require another decision of the Court of Appeal to clarify the effect of *Re Bird Precision Bellows*. See also *Re Castleburn* (1989) 5 B.C.C. 652 and para. 4–052. Compare *Re Abbey Leisure Ltd.* (C.A.), para. 4–054 above.
[41] At p. 222C–D.
[42] It may be that the respondents conceded a "fair value" in argument.

respondents. The court will, however, require the petitioner to show that such an alternative remedy is realistic before allowing the petitioner to proceed. In *Re A Company (No. 003843 of 1986)*[43] the petitioners sought orders, *inter alia*, that they be appointed executive directors at substantial salaries. Millett J. ordered that the petition be stayed, on the ground that this relief was inappropriate in the circumstances of the case, principally because it would be unworkable and the petitioners' real wish was proper financial recompense.[44] In *Re A Company (No. 003096 of 1987)*[45] the petitioners did not accept that they were bound to sell their shares to the respondents upon a breakdown of relations and sought instead a liquidation, alternatively a sale by sealed tender.[46] Peter Gibson J. held that the petition should be struck out, because it was "plain and obvious that petitioners should go" for a number of reasons[47] peculiar to that case.

4–064 The question whether the respondents have made a reasonable offer to the petitioner clearly will be relevant to the fairness of the respondents' conduct. Thus, in *Re A Company (No. 007623 of 1984)*[48] Hoffmann J. held that the exclusion of the petitioner from the business and the proposed rights issue did not amount to unfairly prejudicial conduct because:

(1) in respect of his exclusion, the petitioner had been offered and had accepted a pension; and
(2) in respect of the rights issue, there had been no refusal by the respondents to buy his shares at a fair value to be fixed by the auditors.

Alternative Remedies

4–065 The court is entitled to take into account any alternative remedies available to the petitioner. Indeed, in requiring a petitioner to accept a reasonable offer for his shares or to submit to the procedure of pre-emption provisions in the articles, the court is holding that the petitioner has another, more appropriate, remedy.

The mere fact that the petitioner may have another remedy, for example a common law action for damages based upon the same facts as found the unfair prejudice petition, does not prevent the presentation of the petition: *Re A Company (No. 00477 of 1986)*[49] Nor is an unfair

[43] [1987] B.C.L.C. 562.
[44] At p. 571f–h.
[45] (1988) 4 B.C.C. 80.
[46] See at p. 93. For adverse comments on these remedies see *Re Cumana* [1986] B.C.L.C. 430 (C.A.).
[47] At pp. 93–94. See also *Re Ringtower Holdings plc* (1989) 5 B.C.C. 82,90H. See also *Re A Company (No. 006834 of 1988)* (1989) 5 B.C.C. 218.
[48] [1986] B.C.L.C. 362. See at paras. 4–038 and 4–055 above.
[49] [1986] B.C.L.C. 376; (1986) B.C.C. 99,171.

prejudice petition precluded by the fact that a derivative action might lie in respect of the conduct complained of: *Re A Company*.[50]

Valuation of Shares

4–066 One of the most difficult points in practice in unfair prejudice cases is the proper valuation of shares. In valuing shares, accountants and other experts will have regard to a wide range of factors, such as the net asset value of the company, the profits of the company, the nature of the business and the length of time for which the company has been in operation. These are matters of expert evidence and reference may be made to specialist books on the subject.[51]

The facts of the particular case will, however, render the exercise of valuation a far from exact science. The valuer will need to know:

(1) the date upon which the shares are to be valued;
(2) the basis of valuation, for example a "fair value" or a price as between a willing vendor and willing purchaser, and whether to apply a discount for minority shareholding; and
(3) what allowances have to be made for the unfairly prejudicial conduct which has affected the value of the shares.

4–067 There are two overriding principles in the valuation of shares by the court:

(1) The court has a very wide discretion in determining what is a fair price in all the circumstances of the case.[52]
(2) In determining what is fair and equitable, the court will in general approach the valuation as if the unfairly prejudicial conduct had not taken place.[53] The simplest method of achieving this is to value to shares as at a date prior to the unfairly prejudicial conduct.[54]

4–068 The difference of approaches of the courts in determining whether there has been unfairly prejudicial conduct in the exclusion of a quasi-partner from a quasi-partnership[55] has been continued in the determination of a fair price for the shares in such circumstances. In *Re Bird Precision Bellows Ltd.* Nourse J. held that, in general, the price should

[50] [1986] B.C.L.C. 68. See also *Re Stewarts (Brixton) Ltd.* [1985] B.C.L.C. 4.
[51] See, *e.g.* Eastaway and Booth, *Practical Share Valuation* (2nd ed.).
[52] See *Re London School of Electronics* [1986] Ch. 211; *Re Bird Precision Bellows Ltd.* [1986] Ch. 658, 669D (C.A.).
[53] *Scottish Co-op Wholesale Society* v. *Meyer* [1959] A.C. 324, 364.
[54] See *Re O.C. (Transport) Services Ltd.* [1984] B.C.L.C. 251; *Re A Company (No. 003843 of 1986)* [1987] B.C.L.C. 562.
[55] Para. 4–037 above.

be fixed on a *pro rata* basis without any discount for minority shareholding (in other words as a fraction of the value of the entire issued share capital), if the unfair prejudice had made it intolerable for the petitioner to retain his shareholding.[56] The learned judge contemplated that, if the petitioner had deserved his exclusion, there would have been no unfair prejudice to him.[57] The learned judge added that, if the petitioner was not a quasi-partner but an investor, then a *pro rata* basis of valuation would probably have been inappropriate.[58]

4–069 The distinction drawn in the above case between a quasi-partner participating in management and an investor was analysed in *Re D.R. Chemicals Ltd.*[59] In the circumstances of that case, and in particular the election of the quasi-partner to remain a shareholder for some three years after expulsion, it was held that it was appropriate to apply a discount for a minority shareholding.

4–070 A different approach is manifested in the judgment of Hoffmann J. in *Re A Company (No. 007623 of 1984)*.[60] As has been seen above,[61] in that case it was held that there was no unfair prejudice. If he was wrong in this conclusion, the learned judge held[62] that it was appropriate to apply some discount for a minority holding, but there should also be taken into account the frustration of legitimate expectations as to the receipt of salary. This approach is, on the one hand, more flexible and arguably more realistic but, on the other hand, much more unpredictable.

4–071 The date at which the shares in question are to be valued is also a matter for the discretion of the court in the circumstances of the particular case. In some cases,[63] the date taken has been the date of presentation of the petition, in another case,[64] the date of the order. In the former cases it was suggested that the general principle (if there was such a thing in this context) was that the date of valuation should be the date of presentation of the petition, or the date of unfair prejudice where this was relevant. In the latter case, it was suggested that the date of valuation should be the date of the court's order, because there had been no sea change in the company's business at any material time.

[56] [1984] Ch. 419, 430D–F. Confirmed on appeal: [1986] Ch. 658, 673H–674B. See *Re Abbey Leisure Ltd.*, para. 4–054 above.
[57] At p. 430G–H.
[58] At p. 431C–F.
[59] (1989) 5 B.C.C. 39.
[60] [1986] B.C.L.C. 362.
[61] At para. 4–038 above.
[62] At p. 369.
[63] *Re London School of Electronics* [1986] Ch. 211; *Re Cumana* (*supra*).
[64] *Re D.R. Chemicals Ltd.* (*supra*).

Procedure

The procedure for the presentation and prosecution of a petition under Part XVII of the 1985 Act is expressly governed by the Companies (Unfair Prejudice Applications) Proceedings Rules 1986.[65] Thus: **4–072**

(1) The petition must be in the prescribed form specifying the grounds and the relief sought.
(2) In the High Court,[66] the petition is presented in the Chancery Division Companies Court, and a return date for directions to be given by the Registrar is fixed. No affidavit is necessary.
(3) On the return date, directions will be given for the service of points of claim, etc., or for the service of affidavits.

The following points should be noted: **4–073**

(1) The petition must not be advertised in the London Gazette or elsewhere unless the court specifically so directs. It is highly unlikely that any such direction will be given.
(2) In the case of small private companies, all existing shareholders, whether or not any wrongdoing is alleged or relief is sought against them, should be joined as respondents: *Re A Company (No. 007281 of 1986)*.[67]
(3) It will sometimes bc desirable to consider the submission of particular preliminary points for the determination of the court: for example, whether there has been unfairly prejudicial conduct, if so what remedy is appropriate and, if a share purchase order is appropriate, what basis of valuation should be applied, thus leaving the actual valuation and the calling of expert witnesses to a later hearing if agreement cannot be reached in the meantime.
(4) Before presenting a petition, it is essential to have prepared one's ground carefully, and this will often include having obtained preliminary accountancy advice as to the valuation of the shares. As appears from the above, the court will pay close regard to the open offers that have been made by the parties to one another prior to the petition and the reasonableness of all parties' behaviour.

The individual respondents to the petition are not entitled to use the company's money in their defence.[68] **4–074**

[65] S.I. 1986 No. 2000.
[66] A petition may also be presented in a Chancery district registry (R.S.C., Ord. 9, r. 3), or in a county court. For limitations on the jurisdiction of county courts to make winding-up orders see s. 117 of the 1986 Act. See also para. 3–035.
[67] [1987] B.C.L.C. 593.
[68] *Re Crossmore Electrical & Civil Engineering Ltd.* (1989) 5 B.C.C. 37.

CHAPTER 5

PERSONAL RIGHTS OF SHAREHOLDERS

5–001 As has already been seen in paragraph 2–012 above, the rule in *Foss* v. *Harbottle* embraces the principle that an individual shareholder cannot generally initiate proceedings on behalf of the company. It is clear that this principle can have no application to cases where the individual shareholder is alleging that a wrong has been done to him personally, rather than to the company. In *Edwards* v. *Halliwell,*[1] a case concerning an unincorporated trade union, Jenkins L.J. held:

> "The gist of the case is that the personal and individual rights of membership of each of [the plaintiff members] have been invaded by a purported, but invalid, alteration of the [unions' rules relating to subscriptions payable by its members]. In those circumstances, it seems to me the rule in *Foss* v. *Harbottle* has no application at all, for the individual members who are suing sue, not in the right of the union, but in their own right to protect from invasion their own individual rights as members."[2]

5–002 The recognition that a shareholder's personal rights have been invaded is, however, obviously to be limited by the need to prevent the rule in *Foss* v. *Harbottle* being outflanked. It is implicit in the rule in *Foss* v. *Harbottle* that a company is a person distinct from its members and that a wrong to the company is not in itself a wrong to the shareholders. The recognition of personal rights is also limited by the principle, which has often been regarded (wrongly, it is submitted) as another facet of the rule in *Foss* v. *Harbottle,* that the courts will not interfere in the "internal management" of companies, whatever that might mean.

5–003 There will, however, be cases where individual shareholders suffer personal loss or prejudice to their personal legal interests in the course of

[1] [1950] 2 All E.R. 1064.
[2] [1950] 2 All E.R. 1064, 1067h.

the conduct of the affairs of the company. It may be difficult in some cases to disentangle the loss suffered by the shareholders as distinct from the company and the duties owed to shareholders as distinct from the company.

5–004 The personal rights of shareholders may be said to have been infringed when there has been a breach of the minimal fiduciary duties owed by certain shareholders to others. The circumstances in which the wishes of the majority of shareholders have been set aside for breach of these duties have been examined in Chapter 2 above. The other personal rights with which this chapter is concerned fall into the following categories:

(1) Breach of the company's memorandum or articles of association. If the company, its directors or any of its shareholders are acting in breach of its rules as set out in its memorandum and articles, a shareholder in general can bring proceedings to enforce those rules.
(2) Breach of duty by directors (or, indeed, other shareholders or the company itself) which results in loss or prejudice suffered by the aggrieved shareholder. This is the most contentious area and the law is still in the process of develoment.

Breach of the Memorandum and Articles of Association

5–005 Prima facie, an individual shareholder can bring an action for breach of contract to restrain any proposed breach of the company's memorandum or articles of association or to declare invalid any action based on such a breach. At the root of the rights of an individual shareholder is section 14(1) of the 1985 Act, which provides:

> "(1) Subject to the provisions of this Act, the memorandum and articles of association . . . bind the company and its members to the same extent as if they respectively had been signed and sealed by each member, and contained covenants on the part of each member to observe all the provisions of the memorandum and of the articles."

In general, it may be said, there is no such thing as an article, the breach of which can be waived by a simple majority. If any shareholder or director wishes to act in conflict with the existing memorandum or articles, he must first alter them by special resolution in accordance with the provisions of the 1985 Act[3] or by the procedure provided in the articles themselves.[4]

[3] See ss. 9 and 125 of the 1985 Act.
[4] See para. 6–002 below.

5–006 It is submitted that:

(1) Section 14(1) of the 1985 Act means precisely what it appears to say, namely that the memorandum and articles constitute a contract which is enforceable by an individual shareholder against other shareholders or against the company. Clearly, however, the aggrieved shareholder must be attempting to protect his interests, not those of the company. Examples of the protection afforded to individual shareholders by section 14 are given in paragraph 5–010 below.

(2) The principle stated in (1) above is, however, subject to the overriding rule that the court will not act in vain or determine academic disputes.[5] Suppose, for example, that the articles have been purportedly amended by a special resolution, but a member of the minority claims that the meeting in question was irregularly convened or conducted. It would be pointless for the court to intervene on behalf of the minority if it was clear that the irregularity had been, or would be, cured by a subsequent, regular meeting. This rule of obvious common sense should not, however, be allowed to permit a simple majority of members to conduct the affairs of the company in a manner which would require an alteration to the articles. The extent of this rule is discussed at paragraphs 5–007 onwards.

(3) There is a well-established, if anomalous, rule that shareholders cannot rely on section 14(1) to enforce clauses in the article which do not affect them in their capacity as members. This is discussed at paragraph 5–013 below.

5–007 The principle stated in (1) of the preceding paragraph has in the past been obscured by that stated in (2). Thus, it has sometimes been said that a breach of the articles can only be remedied by the company, not by individual shareholders. A classic example of this confusion is to be found in the judgment of Mellish L.J. in the leading case of *MacDougall* v. *Gardiner*.[6] In that case the company's articles provided that a poll should be taken at a general meeting if demanded by five members. At a general meeting, the chairman ignored a proper demand for a poll and declared that the meeting be adjourned. The meeting had been convened to remove one of the directors and to appoint another, and the requisionists of the meeting had a majority on a poll (when proxies would have been counted) but not on a show of hands. By the time of the hearing before the Court of Appeal, the matter was academic, since the requisionists were in control of the comany and the former directors had resigned. The Court of Appeal dealt, however, with the applicable general principles. Mellish L.J. held:

[5] See, *e.g. Bentley-Stevens* v. *Jones* [1974] 2 All E.R. 653.
[6] (1875) 1 Ch. 13.

"Looking to the nature of these companies, looking at the way in which their articles are formed, and that they are not all lawyers who attend these meetings, nothing can be more likely than that there should be something more or less irregular done at them—some directors may have been irregularly appointed, some directors as irregularly turned out, or something or other may have been done which ought not to have been done according to the proper construction of the articles. Now, if that gives a right to every member of the company to file a bill to have the question decided, then if there happens to be one cantankerous member, or one member who loves litigation, everything of this kind will be litigated; whereas, if the bill must be filed in the name of the company, then, unless there is a majority who really wish for litigation, the litigation will not go on. Therefore, holding that such suits must be brought in the name of the company does certainly greatly tend to stop litigation.

In my opinion, if the thing complained of is a thing which in substance the majority of the company are entitled to do, or if something has been done irregularly which the majority of the company are entitled to do regularly, or if something has been done illegally which the majority of the company are entitled to do legally, there can be no use in having a litigation about it, the ultimate end of which is only that a meeting has to be called, and then ultimately the majority gets its wishes. Is it not better that the rule should be adhered to that if it is a thing which the majority are the masters of, the majority in substance shall be entitled to have their will followed? If it is a matter of that nature, it only comes to this, that the majority are the only persons who can complain that a thing which they are entitled to do has been done irregularly; and that, as I understand it, is what has been decided by the cases of *Mozley* v. *Alston* and *Foss* v. *Harbottle*."[7]

It is submitted that the second paragraph of the above passage is correct, whereas the first paragraph is based on the fallacy that, because some breaches of the articles can be regularised by the majority, therefore all breaches can only be wrongs to the company.

5–008 In *Edwards* v. *Halliwell*,[8] a trade union, whose rules provided for an increase of subscriptions with the consent of a two-thirds majority of members, had purported to increase subscriptions without such consent. In an oft-cited judgment, Jenkins L.J. referred to "the reluctance of the court to interfere with the domestic affairs of a company or association on the ground of mere irregularity in form in the conduct of those affairs"

[7] At p. 25.
[8] [1950] 2 All E.R. 1064.

and held that the breach of the union's rules was not a mere matter of form but one of substance.[9] He then held:

> "The rule in *Foss* v. *Harbottle* . . . comes to no more than this. First, the proper plaintiff in an action in respect of a wrong alleged to be done to a company or association of persons is prima facie the company or the association of persons itself. Secondly, where the alleged wrong is a transaction which might be made binding on the company or association and on all its members by a simple majority of the members, no individual member of the company is allowed to maintain an action in respect of that matter for the simple reason that, if a mere majority of the members of the company or association is in favour of what has been done, then *cadit quaestio*. No wrong has been done to the company or association and there is nothing in respect of which anyone can sue."[10]

It is submitted, however, that it is confusing to categorise cases where the impugned transaction is *ultra vires* the company or required the sanction of a special resolution as exceptions to the rule in *Foss* v. *Harbottle* on the basis that, by definition, they could not be sanctioned by an ordinary resolution. It is submitted that these cases are not cases of wrongs to the company at all but are simply examples of breaches of the company's memorandum and articles where thc court will intervene on the basis of the contract created by section 14(1) of the 1985 Act.

5–009 Other examples of breaches of the articles which can be regularised by the company and therefore do not give rise to a cause of action in an individual shareholder appear from the judgment of Harman L.J. in *Bamford* v. *Bamford:*

> "It is trite law, I had thought, that if directors do acts, as they do every day, especially in private companies, which, perhaps because there is no quorum, or because their appointment was defective, or because sometimes there are no directors properly appointed at all, or because they are actuated by improper motives, they go on doing for years, carrying on the business of the company in the way in which, if properly constituted, they should carry it on, and then they find that everything has been so to speak wrongly done because it was not done by a proper board, such directors can, by making a full and frank disclosure and calling together the general body of the shareholders, obtain absolution and forgiveness of their sins; and provided the acts are not ultra vires the company as a whole everything will go on as if it had been done all right from the beginning."[11]

[9] At p. 1066b–d.
[10] At p. 1066g–h.
[11] [1970] 1 Ch. 212, 238H–239B. See at paras. 5–022 and 5–023 below.

5–010 Where breaches of articles cannot be regularised, an individual shareholder can bring an action to protect his interests. In *Rayfield* v. *Hands* [12] the company's articles required the shareholder/directors to purchase an outgoing member's shares. The court held that it would, if necessary, make an order for specific performance in favour of the latter against the former. In *Quin & Axtens Ltd.* v. *Salmon*[13] the company's articles provided that the company's business should be managed by the board and that no decision of the board should be valid on the relevant issue if either of two particular directors dissented. Farwell L.J. held:

> "... [I]t appears to me to be plain that this [clause in the articles] is a contract by which the business of the company shall be managed by the board. The articles, by [the predecessor of section 14 of the 1985 Act], are made equivalent to a deed of covenant signed by all the shareholders. The Act does not say with whom that covenant is entered into, and there have no doubt been varying statements by learned judges, some of them saying it is with the company, some of them saying it is both with the company and with the shareholders. Stirling J. in *Wood* v. *Odessa Waterworks Co.* (1889) 42 Ch.D. 636,642 says: 'The articles of association constitute a contract not merely between the shareholders and the company, but between each individual shareholder and every other.' I think that that is accurate subject to this observation, that it may well be that the Court would not enforce the covenant as between individual shareholders in most cases."[14]

In the *Salmon* case, an injunction was granted to the aggrieved shareholder/director preventing the company and the majority shareholder from acting upon a resolution of the board and members which did not satisfy the relevant article. The final sentence of the passage cited above is, it would appear, a reference to the principle stated in (2) in paragraph 5–006 above.

5–011 An individual shareholder can enjoin the company from acting in a manner which is *ultra vires* the company.[15] Where, however, it is the company, as opposed to the shareholder, which suffers the financial loss as a result of an *ultra vires* transaction, then an individual shareholder cannot bring an action to recover that loss, unless he can bring a derivative action, because he would not be seeking to protect his personal

[12] [1960] Ch. 1. See also *Heron International* v. *Grade* [1983] B.C.L.C. 244; *Tett* v. *Phoenix* [1986] B.C.L.C. 149.

[13] [1909] 1 Ch. 311; [1909] A.C. 442. See also, *e.g. Heron International* v. Grade [1983] B.C.L.C. 244.

[14] [1909] 1 Ch. 311, 318.

[15] See, *e.g. Simpson* v. *Westminster Palace Hotel* (1860) 8 H.L.C. 712. See also *Smith* v. *Croft* (No. 2) [1988] Ch. 114.

interests in such an action. In *Smith* v. *Croft (No. 2)*[16] it was alleged that the company had suffered loss as a result of an *ultra vires* transaction perpetrated by the majority shareholders/directors. Knox J. accepted the plaintiff's argument that an action to recover such loss was different from an action to recover loss suffered as a result of a director's breach of fiduciary duty, since it was impossible in the former case for any majority of shareholders to ratify the wrongful act retrospectively.[17] As has been noted above,[18] the issue of the ratifiability of the act in question is, it is submitted, a red herring. The crucial question is: is there any reason why the decision of the majority of the shareholders not to sue in respect of a wrong to the company should be overridden? On that issue, Knox J. held that there was no difference between the action before him and any other derivative action.

5–012 The court will enforce the memorandum and articles of a company on the application of a shareholder by injunction or declaration. If the articles vest certain financial rights in a shareholder, such as a right to receive a dividend, then the court will of course enforce those rights against the company. It is nevertheless often said[19] that the court will not award damages against the company or a member in the event of another member suffering loss as a result of a breach of the articles. There is no authority on this issue. It is, however, difficult to see why a shareholder who suffers personal financial loss, as distinct from loss suffered by the company, as a result of a breach of the articles, which loss is not too remote on ordinary contractual principles, should be denied a remedy in damages.

5–013 In the early years of company law there was considerable uncertainty as to the precise effect of what is now section 14(1) of the 1985 Act, and there emerged a curious rule, which appears to have survived to this day, that shareholders cannot rely on that section to enforce rights in the company's articles which do not affect them in their capacity as members. The best known statement of this rule is to be found in the judgment of Astbury J. in *Hickman's Case*:

> " . . . I think this much is clear, first, that no article can constitute a contract between the company and a third person; secondly, that no right merely purporting to be given by an article to a person, whether a member or not, in a capacity other than that of a member, as, for instance, as solicitor, promoter, director, can be enforced against the company; and, thirdly, that articles regulating the rights and obligations of the members generally as such do create rights and obligations between them and the company respectively . . . "[20]

[16] [1988] Ch. 114.
[17] See, *e.g.* at p. 177C.
[18] See at para. 2–018.
[19] See, *e.g.* Gower's *Principles of Modern Company Law,* p. 316.
[20] [1915] 1 Ch. 881.

5–014 The above rule limiting the enforceability of the articles has been subject to much academic debate and is not easy to reconcile with the leading House of Lords decision in *Quin & Axtens Ltd.* v. *Salmon*.[21] In that case, as has already been seen,[22] the company's articles provided that no decision of the board of directors should be valid on the relevant issue if either of two particular directors dissented. Articles to such effect are a common method of protecting the interests of a minority shareholder. It was held that the aggrieved director/shareholder could enjoin the company from acting upon a resolution of the board and the members which did not satisfy the relevant article. This decision may be seen as a forerunner of more recent cases such as *Re Westbourne Galleries*,[23] which decline to recognise a distinction between the rights of shareholders as members and as directors in small companies. The rule stated in *Hickman's Case* nevertheless appears to linger on,[24] so that the moral must be that, in cases of doubt whether an article affects a member in his capacity of a member or in some other capacity, it is prudent to incorporate the provision in a separate contract between the company and the member in question. In that event, not only would there be no doubt as to the enforceability of the contract but also the contract would not be subject to alteration in the same manner as the company's articles, unless it was an express or implied term of the contract that it should be alterable in that way.[25]

Duties Owed by Directors to Shareholders Personally

5–015 It is trite law that the directors of a company owe a number of fiduciary duties to the company. The directors are in a similar, though not identical, position to that of trustees in relation to their beneficiaries. Their beneficiary is generally the company, rather than each and every shareholder individually. This general proposition is assumed to be true in all the cases regarded as "exceptions to the rule in *Foss* v. *Harbottle*,"[26] and, indeed, the justifications for that rule (such as the need to avoid multiplicity of actions, the separate legal personality of the company, and the principle of majority rule) are the same justifications that exist for the above general proposition. There is the further justification that the individual shareholders will generally suffer no loss if the company is able to recover the loss suffered by the general body of shareholders as a group.

5–016 Authority for the above paragraph is contained in *Prudential Assurance* v. *Newman Industries (No. 2)*.[27] The facts of that case are summarised at paragraph 2–027 above. The Court of Appeal held:

[21] [1909] A.C. 442.
[22] See para. 5–011 above.
[23] See para. 3–016 above.
[24] See para. 6–007 below.
[25] See, *e.g. Cumbrian Newspapers* v. *Cumberland Newspaper* [1986] B.C.L.C. 286.
[26] See para. 2–012 below.
[27] [1982] Ch. 204.

> "A personal action would subvert the rule in *Foss* v. *Harbottle* and that rule is not merely a tiresome procedural obstacle placed in the path of a shareholder by a legalistic judiciary. The rule is the consequence of the fact that a corporation is a separate legal entity. Other consequences are limited liability and limited rights. The company is liable for its contracts and torts; the shareholder has no such liability. The company acquires causes of action for breaches of contract and for torts which damage the company. No cause of action vests in the shareholder. When the shareholder acquires a share he accepts the fact that the value of his investment follows the fortunes of the company and that he can only exercise his influence over the fortunes of the company by the exercise of his voting rights in general meeting. The law confers on him the right to ensure that the company observes the limitations of its memorandum of association and the right to ensure that other shareholders observe the rule, imposed upon them by the articles of association. If it is right that the law has conferred or should in certain restricted circumstances confer further rights on a shareholder the scope and consequences of such further rights require careful consideration."[28]

5–017 Earlier in the same judgment, however, the Court of Appeal had recognised that directors of a company might in certain circumstances owe duties to shareholders, although the shareholders had no cause of action for breach of those duties if they suffered no loss distinct from that of the company:

> "It is of course correct, as the judge found and Mr. Bartlett did not dispute, that he and Mr. Laughton [the alleged wrongdoing directors] in advising the shareholders to support the resolution approving the agreement, owed the shareholders a duty to give such advice in good faith and not fraudulently. It is also correct that if directors convene a meeting on the basis of a fraudulent circular, a shareholder will have a right of action to recover any loss which he has been personally caused in consequence of the fraudulent circular; this might include the expense of attending the meeting. But what he cannot do is to recover damages merely because the company in which he is interested has suffered damage. He cannot recover a sum equal to the diminution in the market value of his shares, or equal to the likely diminution in dividend, because such a 'loss' is merely a reflection of the loss suffered by the company. The shareholder does not suffer any personal loss. His only 'loss' is through the company, in the diminution in the value of the net assets of the company, in which he has (say) a 3 per cent. shareholding. The plaintiff's shares

[28] At p. 224A–D.

are merely a right of participation in the company on the terms of the articles of association. The shares themselves, his right of participation, are not directly affected by the wrongdoing. The plaintiff still holds all the shares as his own absolutely unencumbered property. The deceit practised upon the plaintiff does not affect the shares; it merely enables the defendant to rob the company."[29]

5–018 The overriding principle, therefore, is that individual shareholders have no cause of action, unless they can show loss suffered by them personally distinct from the loss suffered by the company. Whereas, generally, an individual shareholder will suffer no such loss as a result of a breach of fiduciary duty by the directors, in certain circumstances he may do so, and in those circumstances it is submitted that there is no reason why the directors should not be held to owe that shareholder a fiduciary duty.

5–019 It is, however, sometimes[30] stated that the directors owe no fiduciary duties to individual shareholders on the authority of *Percival* v. *Wright*.[31] In that case the directors were negotiating for the sale of the company's undertaking to a third party and, without disclosing this fact, accepted the offer of several shareholders to sell their shares at a stated price. The shareholders in question subsequently learnt of the negotiations (which were abortive) and sought to rescind the sale of their shares. Swinfen-Eady J. rejected their claim, but it is noteworthy that he did so, not on the ground that the directors' duty to the company precluded any duty to the shareholders in question, but on the ground that there had been no breach of duty in that case. It is arguable[32] that this case was wrongly decided on its facts, but it is submitted that this case supports the proposition that directors do owe duties to individual shareholders if there is a close enough nexus between the actions of the directors and the individual interests of shareholders.

5–020 Such a nexus was established in *Allen* v. *Hyatt*[33] and *Coleman* v. *Myers*.[34] In the former case the directors were negotiating the amalgamation of the company with a third party and, representing in effect that they would act as agents for the shareholders concerned, took options from these shareholders to purchase their shares. In the event, the directors exercised the options at a profit and claimed to be entitled to retain that profit. Not surprisingly, the Privy Council rejected that claim and found in favour of the shareholders. In the latter case, the facts were

[29] At pp. 222G–223C.
[30] See, *e.g.* Gower's *Principles of Modern Company Law* (4th ed.), p. 573.
[31] [1902] 2 Ch. 421.
[32] See the criticism in *Coleman* v. *Myers* [1977] 2 N.Z.L.R. 225, 298.
[33] (1914) 30 T.L.R. 444.
[34] [1977] 2 N.Z.L.R. 225, 298.

less extreme, but nevertheless unusual. The company was a family company, in which the majority shareholders persuaded the minority shareholders to sell out to them. In the New Zealand Supreme Court Woodhouse J. held that "the standard of conduct required from a director in relation to dealings with a shareholder will differ depending upon all the surrounding circumstances and the nature of the responsibility which in a real and practical sense the director has assumed towards the shareholder."[35] Cooke J. rested his judgment on general equitable principles which govern the circumstances in which a fiduciary relationship arises because of such considerations as undue influence, trust and confidence, and inequality of bargaining power.[36]

5–021 All three cases referred to in the previous paragraph concerned direct dealings between directors and shareholders in the shares of the company.[37] Where there is no such direct dealing, for example where the directors are acting in the course of their duties as such and not in a private capacity as well, it will be much more difficult to establish the existence of a fiduciary relationship with individual shareholders. It is submitted, however, that the law is moving towards the recognition of such a relationship in what may loosely be described as contested takeover situations. Suppose that a shareholder or an outsider makes an offer to buy out the other shareholders in the company. The directors may be obliged or tempted to give advice to shareholders in relation to the offer, and the position of the directors may be complicated by the appearance of a competing bid. The duties of directors in such cases have been considered in several cases.[38] In summary, the directors are not allowed to issue shares for the dominant purpose of creating a new majority—such conduct on their part would be the exercise of their powers for an improper motive. Furthermore, if they become involved in the negotiations, and especially if they are shareholders themselves, they must attempt to obtain the best price available for shareholders. The particular circumstances of the case may give rise to other duties. The relationship between the directors and the shareholders is not as close as in the cases considered in the previous paragraph but it is closer than that existing generally in the directors' performance of their duties as such. In particular, any harm done by the actions of the directors is likely to be suffered by the individual shareholders, and it is somewhat artificial to speak of the directors' duty to act in the interests of the company in such circumstances.

[35] At p. 324.
[36] See, *e.g. Snell's Principles of Equity* (28th ed.), pp. 539–545.
[37] This area of the law is now to some extent governed by the Company Securities (Insider Dealing) Act 1985, to which reference should be made.
[38] See para. 4–044 above. See also *Punt* v. *Symons* [1903] 2 Ch. 506; *Piercy* v. *Mills* [1920] 1 Ch. 77; *Hogg* v. *Cramphorn* [1967] Ch. 254; *Bamford* v. *Bamford* [1970] Ch. 212; *Smith* v. *Ampol* [1974] A.C. 821; and *Heron International* v. *Grade* [1983] B.C.L.C. 244.

5–022 In *Bamford* v. *Bamford*[39] a third party which was supported by substantial but minority shareholders in the company made an offer to buy the shares in the company. The directors responded in a hostile fashion by issuing shares to a customer who would no doubt have supported the status quo. On the trial of a preliminary issue, it was assumed that the directors had acted in bad faith. The Court of Appeal held that the members in general meeting by a simple majority could ratify the voidable issue of shares. It follows from this authority that the directors' duties were owed exclusively to the company, because otherwise there could have been no question of ratification by the members. It is to be noted, however, that the plaintiff's argument in that case took a course that did not impress the Court of Appeal and that it was not argued that any duty was owed to the shareholders personally.

5–023 It is illuminating to compare *Bamford* v. *Bamford*, and the similar earlier case of *Hogg* v. *Cramphorn*,[40] with the subsequent decision of the Court of Appeal in *Heron International* v. *Grade*.[41] This decision is principally an example of the enforcement of the company's articles on the application of an individual (and minority) shareholder. The Court declared that an agreement reached between the directors and a bidder for the company was void because, to the knowledge of the bidder, it infringed an article which restricted the price at which voting shares could be sold for by reference to the market value of the quoted non-voting shares.[42] It is, however, for the Court's observations on the duties owed by the directors to shareholders that this decision is most notable. The Court assumed that a shareholder in a contested takeover situation would have a personal cause of action against the directors if they acted in breach of their fiduciary duties *and the shareholder suffered loss distinct from any loss suffered by the company*.[43] Given the very unusual form of the company's articles and the fact that a takeover was desirable and probably inevitable, the Court concluded that the directors were under a duty, when deciding to whom to sell their shares, to sell them at "the best price reasonably obtainable."[44] The Court held that the directors had not acted in breach of that duty.[45] Events had, however, moved on since the actions in question, and so far as the future was concerned the Court clearly considered that the directors should come to a different conclusion, in the light of their above duty to the current shareholders of the company.[46]

[39] See n. 38.
[40] See n. 38.
[41] See n. 38.
[42] See at pp. 260–261 and 271.
[43] See at pp. 261F–263E.
[44] See at pp. 264F and 265E–H.
[45] See at pp. 269I and 271A–B.
[46] See at p. 271D–I.

It is submitted that the above decision is authority for the proposition that, in a take-over battle where the directors' actions are likely to have a direct effect on the price that the shareholders are likely to be offered, then the directors in exercising their powers may owe a duty to the shareholders individually. On the particular facts of that case, that duty was to obtain an offer for the shares at the best price reasonably attainable. On the facts of *Bamford* v. *Bamford*, it is arguable that the directors' duty to allot shares for a proper purpose was a duty owed to the shareholders individually because the improper allotment had a direct effect, not on the company or any of its assets, but on the price obtainable for the shares. The result of the meeting of shareholders in that case showed, however, that the majority had no intention of accepting the bid, so that the aggrieved minority could not show that it had suffered any loss.

5–024 In *Re Sherborne Park Residents Co. Ltd.*[47] Hoffmann J. held that the directors' fiduciary duty to issue shares for a proper purpose was owed to the shareholders, not the company:

> "Although the alleged breach of fiduciary duty by the board is in theory a breach of its duty to the company, the wrong to the company is not the substance of the complaint. The company is not particularly concerned with who its shareholders are. The true basis of the action is an alleged infringement of the petitioner's individual rights as a shareholder. The allotment is alleged to be an improper and unlawful exercise of the powers granted to the board by the articles of association, which constitute a contract between the company and its members. . . . An abuse of these powers is an infringement of the member's contractual rights under the articles."[48]

It is submitted that this passage, in so far as it states that the duty is owed to the shareholders rather than the company, is supported by the decision in *Heron International* v. *Grade*, although the underpinning of this duty in the articles may be open to further argument.

5–025 In contrast, in *Dawson International* v. *Coats Paton*,[49] it was held by the Court of Session, Outer House, that a board of directors had power, without being in breach of any fiduciary duty, to enter into an agreement with a proposed bidder for the company to the effect that it would recommend the bidder's offer and would not seek or co-operate with alternative bidders. The action arose out of the board's endorsement of an alternative bid. Lord Cullen held that a company could have an

[47] (1986) 2 B.C.C. 99,528. See para. 4–021 above.
[48] At 99,530–99,531.
[49] [1989] B.C.L.C. 233.

interest in the identity of its shareholders on a take-over.[50] The learned judge went on to hold that directors in general owed no fiduciary duty to shareholders with respect to the disposal of their shares in the most advantageous way.[51] The classical approach of the learned judge is captured in the following passage in his judgment:

> "What is in the interests of current shareholders who are sellers of their shares may not necessarily coincide with what is in the interests of the company. The creation of parallel duties could lead to conflict. Directors have but one master, the company."[52]

It is submitted, however, that such classicism must yield to the particular facts of a case. The learned judge acknowledged, however, that the directors might render themselves liable to shareholders if they took it upon themselves to give advice to shareholders.[53] He distinguished *Heron International* v. *Grade*[54] on the basis that it decided, in its peculiar circumstances, that the directors' "duty to consider the interests of the company . . . resolved itself into a duty to have regard to the current shareholders."[55]

5–026 Contested take-over battles in the case of companies listed on the Stock Exchange often give rise to complexities and it is a fair guess that English courts are not keen to enter the fray, especially on an interlocutory basis before the dust has settled. The London Stock Exchange has its own rules and institutions for dealing with take-overs. The principles which the courts will apply have yet to be established.

[50] At pp. 242I–243C.
[51] At p. 243F–I.
[52] At p. 243H.
[53] At pp. 243I–244B.
[54] See para. 5–023 above.
[55] At p. 244C–H.

CHAPTER 6

MISCELLANEOUS RIGHTS OF INDIVIDUAL SHAREHOLDERS

There are a number of provisions in the 1985 Act which are intended to protect the interests of individual shareholders. **6–001**

Alteration of the Memorandum or Articles of Association of the Company **6–002**

The rule, enshrined in sections 4 and 9 of the 1985 Act, that nothing in the memorandum or articles of association can in general be altered without the sanction of a special resolution of the company in general meeting, is fundamental to the position of individual shareholders. On the one hand, this rule prevents a simple majority of members from effecting such an alteration. On the other hand, it is an exception to the general principle that contracts (in the present context the contract created by section 14 of the 1985 Act) cannot be varied without the unanimous consent of the parties thereto.

Alterations to the company's objects are only permitted, in theory at least, for the purposes set out in section 4 of the 1985 Act. In practice, these purposes are so wide as not to impose any limitation. Even if the necessary special resolution for the alteration of the objects is carried, holders of not less than 15 per cent. in nominal value of the issued share capital can apply to the court for an order cancelling the alteration. On such application the court has power to order that the dissentient shareholders be bought out.[1] **6–003**

Alterations to the company's memorandum, other than the objects and other provisions which have to be contained in the memorandum,[2] may generally be made by special resolution for any purpose, but are subject to the same procedure for cancellation.[3] **6–004**

[1] See s. 5 of the 1985 Act.
[2] See s. 2 of the 1985 Act.
[3] See s. 17 of the 1985 Act.

6–005 Subject to the special protection which is accorded to the rights of classes of shareholders,[4] alterations to the articles may be made by special resolution, and, unlike the case of alterations to the memorandum, there is no provision for cancellation by the court.[5] It is possible, however, to make parts of the articles unalterable by inserting them in the memorandum and providing in the memorandum that they are not to be altered. Thus, certain parts of the memorandum can be entrenched. This entrenchment of rights is permitted by the combined effect of section 9(1), which provides that the power to alter the articles is subject to the conditions in the memorandum, and section 17(2)(b), which provides that the power to alter conditions in the memorandum which could have been contained in the articles does not apply

> " . . . where the memorandum itself provides for or prohibits the alteration of all or any of the conditions above referred to, and does not authorise any variation or abrogation of the special rights of any class of members."[6]

Shareholders' rights can also be entrenched by a private agreement amongst shareholders. For example, all the present shareholders of a company could agree that none of them would vote in favour of a variation of specified articles, and there would appear to be no reason why a court should not enforce such an agreement by injunction or otherwise, unless it conflicted with a specific statutory provision.[7] There might be difficulties in enforcing such an agreement against successors in title to the shares.[8]

6–006 Class Rights

The power to vary rights of particular classes of shareholders (in other words, those rights the possession of which distinguish certain shareholders as a class) was clarified by section 32 of the 1980 Act, a revised

[4] See para. 6–006. [5] See s. 9 of the 1985 Act.
[6] It should be noted that a provision in the articles which purports to make certain parts unalterable will be ineffective: see *Walker* v. *London Tramways* (1879) 12 Ch.D. 705; *Allen* v. *Gold Reefs* [1900] 1 Ch.D. 656. Furthermore, it appears that a contract not to alter the articles will not be enforced by injunction against the company, but a breach of such a contract will give rise to a remedy in damages: *Southern Foundries (1926) Ltd.* v. *Shirlaw* [1940] A.C. 701. But see *Cumbrian Newspapers* v. *Cumberland Newspaper* [1986] B.C.L.C. 286, 305h–306d. In this case, Scott J. held, *obiter*, that a company might be enjoined from initiating an alteration of the articles by convening a meeting for that purpose, but no injunction would be granted against the company from convening such a meeting or against members from convening such a meeting pursuant to a members' requisition. Compare s. 303 of the 1985 Act and *Bushell* v. *Faith* [1970] A.C. 1099. Other ways of entrenching provisions in the articles are: (1) to create a special class of shares whose rights can only be varied by special resolution of that class; and (2) to give shareholders weighted voting rights on specific matters.
[7] Such as s. 303 of the 1985 Act. [8] See Appendix para. 7–008.

version of which is now sections 125 to 127 of the 1985 Act. In summary, the current law is as follows:

(1) If the class rights are defined in the articles and the articles contain no provision for the variation of those rights, the rights may be varied by the consent in writing of three-quarters in nominal value of the issued shares of that class or by an extraordinary resolution passed at a meeting of the members of the class. If the memorandum or articles impose any requirement in relation to such a variation, that requirement must be complied with.[9]

(2) If the class rights are defined in the memorandum and neither the memorandum nor the articles contain any provision for the variation of those rights, the rights cannot be varied save with the unanimous consent of all the members of the company.[10]

(3) If the class rights are defined in the memorandum and the articles at the time of incorporation contained (and the articles still contain) provision for their variation, *or* if the class rights are defined in the articles and the articles contain such provision, the rights may only be varied in accordance with such provision.[11]

6–007 Where the rights attached to any class of shares are varied pursuant to a provision in the memorandum or articles or pursuant to the statutory power summarised in sub-paragraph (1) of paragraph 6–006, then dissentient shareholders holding at least 15 per cent. of the relevant shares can apply to the court to cancel the variation. The court can disallow the variation "if satisfied having regard to all the circumstances of the case that the variation would unfairly prejudice the shareholders of the class represented by the applicant."[12]

6–008 It might be thought that a "class" of shareholders would only exist if the articles expressly divided the shares into different classes with different rights. Thus, there might be preference shares with a preferential right to the receipt of dividends on the one hand and ordinary shares with no special rights on the other hand. This is probably too narrow a view. For example, it may be wished to give a particular shareholder special voting rights on some issues. So long as he held those shares, it would appear correct to regard that shareholder as a separate class, for it would only have been a matter of drafting to call his shares by a special name and to have attached special rights to those shares so long as he held them. In *Cumbrian Newspapers* v. *Cumberland Newspaper*[13] the

[9] s. 125(2) of the 1985 Act.
[10] s. 125(5) of the 1985 Act.
[11] s. 125(4) of the 1985 Act. *N.B.* s. 125(3)(c).
[12] See s. 127 of the 1985 Act. It is difficult to see what s. 127(4) adds to the powers that the court has in any event under ss. 459, etc., of the 1985 Act, under which the applicant would not need to have the support of any specified proportion of the class in question.
[13] See n. 6 above.

relevant article of a company provided that a named shareholder had the right of pre-emption in respect of any proposed transfer of shares. Scott J. held that section 125 was intended to provide a comprehensive code for the variation of class rights,[14] and he analysed rights contained in the articles into three categories:

(1) Rights annexed to particular shares. It was common ground that such shares constituted a "class." This category did not apply in that case because the rights attached to a particular person, not particular shares.
(2) Rights conferred on individuals in their capacity other than shareholders. The learned judge held that such rights did not create a "class" of shares, although it is interesting to note that he was prepared to take a broad view of what might constitute interests in the capacity of a member. Thus, if an article, as part of a broad arrangement on the establishment of a quasi-partnership, conferred a right on the holder of certain shares to be the company's solicitor, that right might arguably be regarded as conferred in his capacity as shareholder.[15] In the present case, it was conceded that the rights in question were conferred on the shareholder in his capacity as such.
(3) Rights conferred on a shareholder in his capacity as such but not attached to any particular shares. In the present case, the rights fell into this third category, and were enforceable so long as the plaintiff held any shares in the company. The learned judge, after reviewing the history of section 125 of the 1985 Act, concluded that rights in the third category did give rise to a "class" of shares. Thus, it was not possible to vary these rights by special resolution of the general body of shareholders.

6–009 It will usually be clear whether any proposed variation of the articles will constitute a variation of rights attaching to a class of shares. Sometimes, however, it will not be clear. In the latter type of case, the courts have tended to apply a restrictive test of what constitutes a variation of class rights. For example, it is not sufficient that the holders of the class shares can show a diminution in the value of their shares or prejudice to them in a business sense. If it is desired to protect a class against a particular variation in the structure of the company (for example, a new issue of shares), it would be prudent to entrench that right as an express class right. In *White* v. *Bristol Aeroplane*[16] the issue was whether a bonus issue consisting of ordinary and preference shares to

[14] At pp. 297a and 303c–304b.
[15] See para. 5–014 above.
[16] [1953] Ch. 65.

the ordinary shareholders "affected, modified, varied, dealt with, or abrogated in any manner" the rights of existing preferential shareholders. The Court of Appeal held not, on the basis that, although the voting power of the preferential shares might be diminished by the bonus issue, there was no effect on the rights of the preference shares, but only an effect on the exercise thereof.

Financial Assistance for and the Purchase of a Company's Shares — 6–010

When a private company passes a special resolution to permit itself to give financial assistance for the purchase of its own shares pursuant to section 155 of the 1985 Act, the holders of not less than 10 per cent. in nominal value of the issued shares can apply to the court for the cancellation of that resolution, and the court has power to require the purchase of the dissentient shareholders' interests.[17] When a private company passes a special resolution approving the purchase of its shares out of capital pursuant to section 173 of the 1985 Act, any shareholder can apply to the court for the cancellation of the resolution.[18] Again, the court has power to require the purchase of the shares of the dissentients.

Take-over Bids — 6–011

Sections 428 to 430F of the 1985 Act[19] provide a mechanism whereby a person making a take-over bid for a company's shares can, having received acceptances from 90 per cent. of the holders of relevant shares, compulsorily acquire the remaining shares. The requirements of the sections must be complied with.[20] Any dissentient shareholder may, however, apply to the court for an order either (1) cancelling the compulsory purchase or (2) specifying different terms of purchase.[21] On such an application, the applicant bears a heavy burden of proving that the terms offered are unfair. Unless the application, however, was

> " . . . unnecessary, improper or vexatious, or [the applicant] has been guilty of unreasonable delay or unreasonable conduct in conducting the proceedings,"

[17] ss. 157(2) and (3) and ss. 54(3)–(10). The latter section grants the holders of at least 5 per cent. of the company's shares the right to apply to the court to object to the re-registration of a public company as a private company.
[18] ss. 176 and 177 of the 1985 Act. There is a time limit of five weeks from the date of the resolution.
[19] As substituted by s. 172 and Sched. 12 to the Financial Services Act 1986 for the old ss. 428–430 of the 1985 Act.
[20] The details thereof are beyond the scope of this book and the reader is referred to the general textbooks on company law.
[21] s. 430C(1). The application must be made within six weeks of the acquisition notice.

the court will not make any order for costs against an unsuccessful applicant. [22] In *Re Bugle Press Ltd.*[23] the majority shareholders of a private company were negotiating to buy the shares of the minority shareholder. When these negotiations broke down, the enterprising majority purported to launch a take-over bid through a company owned by them and attempted to invoke the predecessor of section 428 of the 1985 Act. Evershed M.R. held:

> "It is no doubt true to say that it is still for the minority shareholder to establish that the discretion should be exercised in the way that he seeks . . . but if the minority shareholder does show, as he shows here, that the offeror and the 90 per cent. of the transferor company's shareholders are the same, then as it seems to me he has, prima facie, shown that the court ought otherwise to order, since if it should not do so the result would be . . . that the section has been used not for the purpose of any scheme or contract properly so called or contemplated by the section but for the quite different purpose of enabling majority shareholders to expropriate or evict the minority; and that, as it seems to me, is something for the purposes of which, prima facie, the court ought not to allow the section to be invoked—unless at any rate it were shown that there was some good reason in the interests of the company for so doing, for example, that the minority shareholder was in some way acting in a manner destructive or highly damaging to the interests of the company for some motives entirely of his own."[24]

Thus, in that case it would not have been sufficient that the terms offered to the minority shareholder were fair.[25]

6–012 Section 430A(1) gives a shareholder who has not accepted the offer the right to require the offeror to purchase his shares. The conditions that give rise to such a right are similar, but not identical, to those applicable to the right of compulsory acquisition by the offeror.[26] Where a shareholder exercises this right, either he or the offeror may apply to the court for an order that the terms of the purchase be fixed by the court.[27] The minority shareholder enjoys the same protection as to costs as applies to an application to resist a compulsory purchase of his shares.

[22] s. 430C(4).
[23] [1961] Ch. 270.
[24] At pp. 286–287.
[25] In the court below, Buckley J. had held that in the circumstances the onus lay on the majority to show that the terms were fair and they had not so shown.
[26] It should be noted that, in the case of the right of the minority to be acquired, all the shares held by the offeror are counted in calculating the threshold of acceptances reached.
[27] s. 430C(3).

Department of Trade Investigation **6–013**

The Department of Trade may appoint one or more competent inspectors "to investigate the affairs of a company and to report on them" in the circumstances mentioned in sections 431 and 432 of the 1985 Act. Such an appointment may be made, for example, upon the application either of not less than 200 members or of members holding at least 10 per cent. of the issued shares.[28] The Department of Trade can insist upon the giving of security for the costs of the investigation.[29] The powers of any inspector appointed and of the Secretary of State consequential upon his report are set out in sections 433 to 441 of the 1985 Act. The appointment of an inspector by the Department of Trade is a rare event, particularly in the case of private companies, and it would appear to be highly unlikely that an appointment would be made in cases where there was an essentially domestic dispute between shareholders in a private company, which was amenable to resolution by the ordinary process of litigation.

[28] s. 431(2).
[29] s. 431(4).

Appendix

The purpose of this Appendix is to provide examples of provisions which may be inserted in the memorandum or articles of association of a company, or in an agreement between shareholders in a company, for the protection of a minority shareholder. Every case is different and the contents of the rules of a company and of any shareholders' agreement will necessarily be determined by the circumstances and the bargaining position of the parties. **7–001**

Memorandum of Association

As has been seen in paragraph 6–005 above, the memorandum can be used as a means of entrenching rules and regulations which would otherwise have been alterable if contained in the articles. Conversely, if it is intended to give some protection to minority shareholders, but to make allowance for future change of circumstances, it may be preferable to make provision for that protection in the articles rather than in the memorandum or a shareholders' agreement, since section 125 of the 1985 Act will then supply a procedure for change in the light of those future circumstances. **7–002**

An example of a provision entrenched in the memorandum is as follows[1]: **7–003**

"[4.] (i) Upon any resolution put to members in general meeting in respect of any of the matters specified in sub-paragraph (ii) below, [the holder of the 'S' share] [named shareholder] shall have the right to demand a poll and upon the taking of such a poll shall have such number of votes as shall equal the sum of 1 and the total number of votes held by the holders of shares in the company other than [the holder of the 'S' share] [named shareholder].

[1] It could also have been protected as a class right if inserted in the articles.

(ii) (a) The removal from office as a director of the company of [the holder of the 'S' share] [named shareholder] [or any person appointed director by the said holder] [named shareholder] [pursuant to the provisions of regulation [ ] of the articles of association].
(b) The issue of any shares in the company whether by way of new issue or rights or bonus issue or otherwise howsoever.

(iii) The provisions of this clause are hereby declared to be unalterable save with the prior written consent of the [holder of the "S" share] [named shareholder]."

Articles of association

7–004 *Pre-emption Provisions*

Such provisions are relatively common in the case of private companies, for the obvious reason that they give remaining shareholders the right of first refusal in the case of a proposed sale of shares. For the significance of the contents of pre-emption provisions in unfair prejudice and just and equitable petitions, see paragraphs 4–047 to 4–054 above. The wording of such provisions can be weighted in favour of the majority. For example, the decision as to which shareholders should have the opportunity to purchase the shares on offer might be left to the directors who might be tempted to favour themselves or their associates. To be preferred from the point of view of the minority shareholder is a provision akin to that set out in section 89 of the 1985 Act in the case of new issues. Provisions to the effect that the valuation of the offered shares shall be undertaken by the company auditor at a "fair value" will also tend to favour the majority. To be preferred from the point of view of a minority shareholder are provisions which allow for valuation by an independent valuer on the basis of the value of the block of shares on offer without any discount for a minority shareholding. There would, moreover, appear to be no objection in principle to a provision to the effect that the pre-emption clause was not to be regarded as intended to provide for the case of a shareholder who would otherwise be entitled to a winding-up order on the just and equitable ground or to a share purchase order on the unfair prejudice ground.

7–005 "[ ]. (i) Except in the case of a transfer of shares in accordance with articles [ ] above, no share in the company shall be transferred until the conditions of this clause shall have been complied with.

(ii) Any member proposing to transfer any shares in the company ("the proposed transferor") shall give a notice in writing ("the transfer notice") to the company by lodging the same at the registered office of the company and by sending a copy of the same to the secretary for the time being of the company.

(iii) The transfer notice shall constitute the company by its board of directors as the agent of the proposed transferor for the sale of all (but not part only of) the shares referred to in the transfer notice ("the transfer shares") at the price fixed in accordance with sub-clause (ix) below.
[The transfer notice shall be revocable at any time prior to [the expiry of 7 days after notification of the price fixed as aforesaid] by giving the same notice as required for the notice itself.]

(iv) The directors shall offer the transfer shares to the members of the company other than the proposed transferor in the proportion which is as nearly as practicable equal to the proportion in nominal value held by the said members of the issued capital of the company. If any such member shall not take up his full allocation of shares as aforesaid, the part thereof not taken up shall be offered to the remaining members in the same proportion as aforesaid, and so on until the last remaining shareholder. In the event of any dispute or difficulty as to the entitlement of members pursuant to the above provisions or as to the procedure to be adopted, the same shall be determined by the directors in their absolute discretion. If the members shall not have taken up the offer to sell all of the transfer shares, the directors may offer those shares not taken up as aforesaid to such other person or persons as they shall select.

(v) If within a period of one month after receipt of the transfer notice the company shall have found purchasers for all of the transfer shares, the company shall give notice of such fact and of the names and addresses of the purchasers and of the number of shares purchased by them respectively to the proposed transferor, who shall thereupon become obliged [subject to his right to revoke the transfer notice] upon payment of the price fixed as aforesaid to transfer the transfer shares to the purchasers thereof.

(vi) Within seven days after receipt of the notice referred to in the preceding paragraph, the proposed transferor shall deliver the company the certificate or certificates in respect of the transfer shares and duly execute instruments of transfer in favour of the purchasers thereof. The purchase shall be completed within 28 days after receipt of the said notice or so soon thereafter as is practicable at a time and place and in such manner as shall be determined by the board of directors of the company.

(vii) If the proposed transferor shall default in the performance of his obligations set out in the preceding sub-paragraph, the chairman of the company, or some other person nominated by the board of directors of the company, is hereby granted a power of attorney to execute all such instruments of transfer and other documents on behalf of the proposed transfer and is duly authorised to do all such other things as are necessary to procure the due performance of the said obligations. The receipt of such person for the purchase money for the transfer shares shall be a good discharge to the purchaser or purchasers thereof, and the said purchase money shall be held on trust for the proposed transferor.

(viii) If within a period of one month (being one calendar month inclusive of the date of receipt of the transfer notice and expiring on the first working day following the expiry of the calendar month) the company shall not have sent a notice to the proposed transferor pursuant to sub-paragraph (v) above, the proposed transferor shall be at liberty [subject to the general restrictions as to transfer contained in articles [ ]] [and the directors shall be bound to register any transfer pursuant to such liberty] to transfer all or any of the transfer shares [at whatever price and for whatever consideration (if any)] [at a price per share not less than the price fixed in accordance with sub-paragraph (ix) below].

(ix) The price for the transfer shares shall, in the absence of prior agreement, be fixed by an independent chartered accountant appointed, in the absence of agreement, by the President for the time being of the Institute of Chartered Accountants. The said appointment shall be made and the determination of the said accountant shall be delivered to the company and the proposed transferor as soon as possible after the receipt of the transfer notice. The proposing transferor and any shareholder interested in acquiring any of the transfer shares shall be entitled to submit representations in writing (but not otherwise) to the said accountant within [seven] days after notification of his appointment. The company shall supply to the said accountant all such information relating to its financial position as shall be reasonably requested by the said accountant. The said accountant shall act as an expert and not as an arbitrator and his decision shall be final and binding. He shall not be required, unless he so desires, to give any reasons for his determination. He shall value the transfer shares as at the date of the transfer notice, without any discount for the fact that they may constitute a minority shareholding and without any uplift for the fact that they may constitute a majority shareholding. Subject thereto, the said accountant shall fix what is, in his opinion, the fair value of the transfer shares and he may have regard to all the circumstances that he may consider relevant, including any alleged financial impropriety in relation to the affairs of the company, in fixing the said fair value. The cost of the said valuation shall be borne by the company unless the said accountant shall otherwise direct on the ground of an unreasonable rejection of an offer made either openly or 'without prejudice save as to costs.'

[(x) There shall be deemed to be served a transfer notice in accordance with the provisions of this article in the following circumstances:

(a) The resignation from office as a director of the company or the rightful determination of any contract of employment with the company of any person who shall have been a shareholder of the company at the date of the adoption of these articles.

(b) The establishment by any shareholder of a business which competes with that of the company.

In the event of a deemed service of a transfer notice pursuant to this sub-paragraph, the transfer notice shall comprise all shares registered in the name of or owned beneficially and absolutely by the proposed transferor.]

[*NOTE*: The above sub-paragraph might be considered a restriction on the rights of an individual shareholder. The following sub-paragraph is designed to give the maximum protection to a minority shareholder, although there can be no certainty that a court would give full effect to it.]

[(xi) Under no circumstances whatsoever are the provisions of this article intended to apply if any shareholder would, in the absence of such provisions, have the right to an order under section 461 of the Companies Act 1985 (and any re-enactment or successor thereto) that the company or any shareholder therein shall purchase his shares in the company at a price to be determined by the court, and it is hereby further declared that such right is not liable to be defeated by any offer to purchase his shares at a value to be determined by an independent valuer.]"

7–006 *Class Rights*

"[ ] (i) The 'A' shares shall have the rights set out in this article, but subject thereto they shall rank *pari passu* in all respects with the ordinary shares.

(ii) The 'A' shares shall carry the right as a class to nominate, either in writing signed by or on behalf of a majority of the class or by ordinary resolution of a separate class meeting, one director to the board of directors of the company. Such a nominated director shall hold office until removed in the same manner as he was appointed. Upon any resolution of the company in general meeting to remove the said nominated director the holders of the 'A' shares shall collectively be entitled to such number of votes as shall equal the sum of one and the number of votes held by the holders of the other shares in the company.

(iii) The company shall not enter into any contract of employment with any servant or officer of the company which cannot be determined without penalty to the company (other than such penalty as is prescribed by law) by three months' notice until a draft of the proposed contract has been approved by the board of directors of the company and the director nominated by the 'A' shareholders voted in favour thereof."

7–007 *Deadlock*

"[ ] (i) The share capital of the company shall be divided into 'A'and 'B' shares. Save as is hereinafter provided, the 'A' and 'B' shares shall rank *pari passu* in all respects.

(ii) The holder or holders for the time being of the 'A' and 'B' shares shall have the right as a class respectively to appoint one director to the board of directors of the company. The said class shall have the right to remove such nominated director and to appoint another in his place. Upon any resolution of the Company in general meeting to remove any such nominated director, the holders of the class that nominated him shall be entitled to such number of votes as is equal to the sum of one and the number of votes held by the other shareholders.

(iii) Upon any resolution purporting to vary any of the provisions of this article, any holder of any 'A' or 'B' share desirous of voting against the said resolution shall have such number of votes as is equal to the sum of one and the whole number equal to or nearest to but greater than one quarter of the number of votes held by all the shareholders in the company, provided that the provisions of this article may be varied at the direction of special resolutions of separate class meetings of the 'A' and 'B' shareholders respectively.

(iv) The company shall have no power to enter into any of the following transactions unless the same shall first have been approved by both directors nominated as aforesaid:
   (a) The issue of any shares in the company;
   (b) The payment of any dividends by the company;
   (c) Any transaction which requires the sanction of an ordinary or special resolution under any provision of the Companies Act 1985;
   (d) The giving of any guarantee or any charge over the assets of the company;
   (e) The incurring of any liability to any person other than a wholly owned subsidiary of the company for an amount in excess of £50,000;
   (f) The entry into any contract of employment or of services between the company and any other person which cannot be determined without penalty by the company (other than such penalty as is prescribed by law) by three months' notice to that person; and
   (g) The payment of any directors' fees other than such salary or other remuneration as a director may be contractually entitled to.

(v) If any such nominated director shall decline to approve of any such specified transaction, the other director shall have the right to remit any dispute for determination by the auditors of the company or, if they shall decline to do so, an accountant or solicitor or barrister agreed between the parties or nominated by the President for the time being of the Law Society. For the purpose of this article, if such person shall conclude that the refusal of the nominated director to approve of the transaction in question was unreasonable in all the circumstances, the determination of such person shall be substituted for the decision of the nominated director upon the transaction in question. If such person shall conclude that either (a) the nominated director acted unreasonably in refusing his consent to the transaction or (b) there were insufficient grounds for interference with the nominated director's refusal to give his approval and that in all the circumstances the applicant nominated director has acted unreasonably in the making of this application, he shall so certify. The cost of such determination shall be borne in such manner as such person shall direct. The determination of such person shall be final and binding, need not be accompanied by reasons and shall not be deemed to be an arbitration or otherwise open to legal challenge.

[*NOTE*: A provision in effect for arbitration in the case of deadlock is not novel or one that is likely to solve all disputes: see paragraph 3–025 above.]

(vi) [If in the course of a period of 12 consecutive months it shall be determined by such a person that the director for the time being nominated pursuant to the provisions of this article by either the holders of the 'A' or 'B' shares on [3] occasions acted unreasonably in refusing his consent to a particular transaction or in making an application pursuant to the preceding subparagraph,] the holders of the class of shares in question shall be deemed to have served a transfer notice in respect of all their shares of whatever class pursuant to the provisions of article [ ] above."

Shareholders' Agreement

7–008 As indicated above, the terms of such an agreement are infinitely wide-ranging. Two general clauses are suggested here:

"[ ]. The provisions of this agreement shall bind the parties hereto so long as they are shareholders in the company or have any beneficial interest therein and every party hereto shall further procure that so far as possible every person who shall acquire title to or any beneficial interest in any shares in the company from him whether by transfer or transmission of law or otherwise shall be aware of and agree to be bound by the terms of this agreement as if they were an original party hereto.

[ ]. It is hereby agreed that clauses [ ] to [ ] of the articles of association of the company, a true copy of which are appended to this agreement, shall not in any circumstances be varied except with the unanimous prior written consent of all the shareholders in the company, and to that end the parties hereto undertake to procure that so far as lies within their power all votes of shareholders shall be exercised against any resolution to vary any of the said articles in the absence of such consent."

INDEX

Articles of Association,
  alteration,
    rights, on, 6–002—6–005
    variation of class rights by, 6–009
  breach of,
    academic disputes, 5–006, 5–007
    action, shareholder bringing, 5–010
    company, remedied by, 5–007—5–009
    contract, as, 5–006, 5–008
    enforcement by court, 5–012—5–014, 5–023
    remedy, 5–007
    right of action, 5–005
    ultra vires transactions, 5–008, 5–011
  minority shareholders, provisions protecting,
    class rights, 7–006
    deadlock, as to, 7–007
    pre-emption, 7–004, 7–005
    Shareholders' Agreement, 7–008
  pre-emption. *See* Pre-emption articles
  variation of class rights by, 6–009

Breach of Memorandum and Articles
  academic disputes, 5–006, 5–007
  action, shareholder bringing, 5–010
  company, remedied by, 5–007—5–009
  contract, as, 5–006, 5–008
  enforcement by court, 5–012—5–014, 5–023
  remedy, 5–007
  right of action, 5–005
  ultra vires transactions, 5–008, 5–011

Class rights, variation of
  Articles, protection in, 7–006
  code for, 6–008
  dissentient shareholders, application to cancel, 6–007
  power of, 6–006
  pre-emption rights, 6–008
  variation of articles, by, 6–009
Company
  group, as, 2–005
  member, meaning, 4–002
  objects, alteration of, 6–003
  proceedings on behalf of, 2–012—2–016
Company—*cont.*
  purchase of own shares, financial assistance for, 6–010
  separate from members, being, 2–005
Contributory
  meaning, 3–003
  winding-up petition, presenting, 3–003—3–008

Department of Trade
  investigation by, 6–013
Derivative action
  clean hands, shareholder having, 2–042
  control, degree of, 2–027—2–034
  costs, 2–037—2–039
  meaning, 2–012
  minority shareholder, right to bring, 2–013—2–016, 2–042
  prima facie case, establishment of, 2–036
  procedure, 2–035, 2–036
  shareholders not voting for benefit of company, 2–019
  tainted votes, effect of, 2–020
  unfair prejudice remedy, 2–041
Director
  breakdown of relationship between, 3–026, 3–027
  duties owed by,
    acting in course of, 5–021
    bad faith, acting in, 5–022
    breach of, 5–019
    cause of action, 5–017, 5–018
    direct dealings, in, 5–021
    fiduciary, 5–015
    standard of conduct, 5–020
    take-over battle, in, 5–023—5–026
  excessive remuneration to, 4–041, 4–042
  independent,
    consulting, 2–028—2–033
    costs of action, considering, 2–037—2–039
  loss of confidence, in, 3–022, 3–023
  loss of office, winding-up on ground of, 3–015—3–021
Discrimination
  improper conduct as, 4–045
  minority shareholders, against, 4–031, 4–032

Dividend
  inadequate, payment as unfair prejudice, 4–043
  non-payment as ground for winding-up, 3–028, 3–029

Financial assistance
  purchase of own shares, for, 6–010
Foss v. *Harbottle,* rule in
  concepts dealt with, 1–003
  exceptions,
    cause of action alleged, 2–021—2–026
    control, degree of, 2–027—2–034
    general propositions, 2–017—2–020
    personal rights of shareholders, 2–040, 5–001, 5–002, 5–016
    unfair prejudice, 2–041
  principle of, 2–012
  rights governed by, 1–001
Fraud
  minority, on, 2–043
  power, on, 2–043

Groups, rules governing,
  conflict of interest, 2–003
  expulsion, allowing, 2–002
  independent members, acting for, 2–004
  provisions in, 2–001

Injunction
  discretion, exercise by court, 4–017
  general powers of court, 4–017—4–019
  memorandum and articles, enforcement of, 5–012—5–014
  unfair prejudice, in case of. *See* Unfair prejudice

Joint venture
  management, exclusion from, 4–036—4–049
  rights of members, 4–030
  unfair prejudice to partner in, 4–008, 4–009

Locus standi
  unfair prejudice remedy, for,
    joint venture, partner in, 4–008, 4–009
    member of company, of, 4–002, 4–003
    person erroneously registered, of, 4–010
    person not registered, of, 4–004, 4–008
    person to whom shares transferred, 4–004—4–008

Locus standi—cont.
  winding-up on fair and equitable ground, for,
    contributory, of, 3–003
    disputes over shares, effect of, 3–007, 3–008
    original allottee of shares, of, 3–005, 3–006

Majority rule, exceptions to principle
    companies, 2–005, 2–006
  derivative actions. *See* Derivative action
  general equitable principles,
    benefit of company, action being, 2–008—2–010
    authorities, 2–006, 2–007
    disregard of votes, 2–008
  groups, rules governing,
    conflict of interest, 2–003
    expulsion, allowing, 2–002
    independent members, acting for, 2–004
    provisions in, 2–001
  rule in *Foss* v. *Harbottle. See Foss* v. *Harbottle,* rule in
Memorandum and Articles
  alteration, rights on, 6–002—6–005
  breach of,
    academic disputes, 5–006, 5–007
    action, bringing, 5–010
    company, remedied by, 5–007—5–009
    contract, as, 5–006, 5–008
    enforcement by court, 5–012—5–014
    remedy, 5–007
    right of action, 5–005
    ultra vires transactions, 5–008, 5–011
  provisions protecting minority shareholders, 7–002, 7–003
Minority shareholders
  action by,
    clean hands, having, 2–042
    company in liquidation, 2–034
    costs, 2–037—2–039
    form of, 2–035
    negligence, for, 2–024
    prima facie case, establishment of, 2–036
    procedure, 2–035, 2–036
    right to bring, 2–013—2–016
    ultra vires transaction, to correct, 2–030
  compulsory purchase of shares, 6–012
  discrimination against, 4–031, 4–032
  fraud on, 2–043
  majority decision, complaining of, 2–009
  oppression of, 4–001
  provisions protecting,
    Articles, in, 7–004—7–007

Minority shareholders—*cont.*
provisions protecting—*cont.*
Memorandum, in, 7–002, 7–003
rights,
non-quoted companies, 1–004
procedural questions, 2–004
rule in *Foss* v. *Harbottle*. *See Foss* v. *Harbottle,* rule in
statutory provisions, 1–001, 1–002
unfair prejudice to. *See* Unfair prejudice

Negligence
minority shareholder action for, 2–024

Personal rights of shareholders
directors, duties owed by,
acting in course of, 5–021
bad faith, acting in, 5–022
breach of, 5–019
cause of action, 5–017, 5–018
direct dealings, in, 5–021
fiduciary, 5–015
standard of conduct, 5–020
take-over battle, in, 5–023—5–026
fiduciary duties to, breach of, 5–004
general principles, 2–006, 2–040
loss or prejudice, suffering, 5–003
Memorandum and Articles, breach of,
academic disputes, 5–006, 5–007
action, bringing, 5–010
company, remedied by, 5–007—5–009
contract, as, 5–006, 5–008
enforcement by court, 5–0125–014, 5–023
remedy, 5–007
right of action, 5–005
ultra vires transactions, 5–008, 5–011
rule in *Foss* v. *Harbottle,* exclusion of, 5–001, 5–002
Pre-emption articles
class rights, variation of, 6–008
example of, 7–004, 7–005
provisions in, 4–047
unfair prejudice in respect of,
joint venturers, breakdown between, 4–048, 4–049
minority shareholding, discount for, 4–050
quasi-partnership, in, 4–052, 4–054
rights issue, proposed, 4–047
winding-up on just and equitable ground, and, 3–030
Prejudice. *See* Unfair prejudice

Quasi-partnership
management, exclusion from, 4–039,

Quasi-partnership—*cont.*
pre-emption provisions, 4–052, 4–054
valuation of shares, 4–068, 4–069

Rights of shareholders
class, variation of, 6–006—6–009
concept of, 4–028
Department of Trade investigation, application for, 6–013
extension of, 4–030
legal, restricted to, 4–029
Memorandum and Articles, alteration of, 6–002—6–005
non-quoted companies, 1–004
personal. *See* Personal rights of shareholders
procedural questions, 2–004
purchase of own shares, on, 6–010
rule in *Foss* v. *Harbottle*. *See Foss* v. *Harbottle,* rule in
statutory provisions, 1–001, 1–002
take-over bids, on, 6–011, 6–012
voting, restriction on, 2–006

Shareholders
agreement, 7–008
expectations of, 4–028
indemnification of, 4–021
independent,
consulting, 2–028—2–033
costs of action, considering, 2–037—2–039
minority. *See* Minority shareholders
obligations of, 4–028
personal interests, voting on matters of, 2–021
rights of,
class, variation of, 6–006—6–009
concept of, 4–028
Department of Trade investigation, application for, 6–013
extension of, 4–030
legal, restricted to, 4–029
Memorandum and Articles, alteration of, 6–002—6–005
personal. *See* Personal rights of shareholders
purchase of own shares, on, 6–010
take-over bids, on, 6–011, 6–012
unfair prejudice to. *See* Unfair prejudice
voting rights, restriction on, 2–006
Shares
purchase of own, financial assistance for, 6–010
unfair prejudice, purchase in case of, interim order for, 4–020

Shares—*cont.*
unfair prejudice—*cont.*
order for, 4–013—4–016

Take-over bids
directors, duties of, 5–023—5–026
shareholders, rights of, 6–011, 6–012
unfair prejudice in relation to, 4–044

Ultra vires transactions
action by shareholder, 2–030, 5–008, 5–011
Unfair prejudice
application of test,
business, diversion of, 4–040
excessive remuneration to directors, 4–041, 4–042
improper purposes, conduct for, 4–045, 4–046
inadequate dividends, 4–043
management, exclusion from, 4–036—4–039
pre-emption provisions, 4–047—4–054
take-over bids, 4–044
conduct dehors the company, 4–024
conduct in the company, 4–023
discrimination, 4–031, 4–032
establishment of, 4–022
interests of members, to,
member, as, 4–026, 4–027
rights, expectations and obligations of shareholders, 4–028—4–030
part of members, to, 4–031, 4–032
prejudice, 4–033, 4–034
proposed rights issue as, 4–046, 4–047
remedy. *See* Unfair prejudice remedy
statutory test, 4–022, 4–025—4–035
unfairness, 4–035
Unfair prejudice remedy
costs indemnity, 4–021
court,
alternative remedies, taking into account, 4–065
discretion and powers of, 4–001
final orders, 4–011—4–016
interlocutory orders, 4–017—4–021
status quo, preservation of, 4–019
defence, money used for, 4–074
locus standi,
joint venture, partner in, 4–008, 4–009
member of company, of, 4–002, 4–003
person erroneously registered, of, 4–010
person not registered, of, 4–004, 4–008
person to whom shares transferred, 4–004—4–008
procedure, 4–072—4–074

Unfair prejudice remedy—*cont.*
purchase of shares, *see also* reasonable offers for shares; valuation of shares, *below*
interim order for, 4–020
order for, 4–013—4–016
reasonable offers for shares,
fair value, 4–063
fairness of conduct, and, 4–064
independent valuation, 4–057—5–060
non-discounted basis, on, 4–050, 4–061
open market value, 4–062
petition, effect on, 4–055
remedies, 4–012—4–016
statutory provisions, 4–001
valuation of shares,
date of, 4–071
factors taken into account, 4–006
minority shareholding, discount for, 4–050, 4–061, 4–070
principles, 4–067
quasi-partner, exclusion of, on, 4–068, 4–069
winding-up on just and equitable ground, and, 3–032

Winding-up on just and equitable ground
alternative remedy, existence of, 3–034
dividends, non-payment of, 3–028, 3–029
justification of,
breakdown of relationship between directors, 3–026, 3–027, 3–033
deadlock, in case of, 3–024, 3–025
generally, 3–014
loss of confidence, 3–022, 3–023
office, expulsion from, 3–015—3–021
locus standi,
contributory, of, 3–003
disputes over shares, effect of, 3–007, 3–008
original allottee of shares, of, 3–005, 3–006
minority shareholders' rights, governing, 1–002
other remedies, and, 3–031—3–034
pre-emption articles, and, 3–030
procedure for, 3–035, 3–036
reasonable offer for shares, effect of, 4–056
single shareholder seeking, 3–001
statutory provisions, 3–01, 3–002
tangible interest, proof of, 3–009—3–013
unfair prejudice remedy, and, 3–032
unreasonably pursuing, 3–034